The Holy Spirit
and an Evolving Church

The Holy Spirit
and an Evolving Church

James A. Coriden

ORBIS BOOKS

Maryknoll, New York 10545

Founded in 1970, Orbis Books endeavors to publish works that enlighten the mind, nourish the spirit, and challenge the conscience. The publishing arm of the Maryknoll Fathers and Brothers, Orbis seeks to explore the global dimensions of the Christian faith and mission, to invite dialogue with diverse cultures and religious traditions, and to serve the cause of reconciliation and peace. The books published reflect the views of their authors and do not represent the official position of the Maryknoll Society. To learn more about Maryknoll and Orbis Books, please visit our website at www.maryknollsociety.org.

Manufactured in the United States of America.

Manuscript editing and typesetting by Joan Weber Laflamme.

Scripture quotations are from the New Revised Standard Version of the Bible, copyright © 1989 by the National Council of the Churches of Christ in the USA. All rights reserved.

Library of Congress Cataloging-in-Publication Data

Names: Coriden, James A., author.
Title: The Holy Spirit and an evolving church / James A. Coriden.
Description: Maryknoll : Orbis Books, 2018. | Includes bibliographical references and index.
Identifiers: LCCN 2017036255 (print) | LCCN 2017048273 (ebook) | ISBN 9781608337293 (e-book) | ISBN 9781626982635 (pbk.)
Subjects: LCSH: Holy Spirit. | Church.
Classification: LCC BT121.3 (ebook) | LCC BT121.3 .C67 2018 (print) | DDC 231/.3—dc23
LC record available at https://lccn.loc.gov/2017036255

Contents

Introduction

The Holy Spirit and the Church

The Holy Spirit is the soul of the church. The Spirit gives life, unity, and movement to the whole body, just as the soul is the life principle of the human body. The Spirit functions as the vital source of all of the church's activities.

The Holy Spirit sanctifies the church and dwells in the hearts of the faithful as in a temple. In the sacraments of initiation the Spirit makes the catechumens the adopted children of God. The Spirit sanctifies the eucharistic gifts so that they become the body and blood of our Lord Jesus Christ. The Spirit brings the forgiveness of sins.

The Holy Spirit preserves the church in truth. The indwelling Spirit leads the church into all truth and declares to us what Jesus taught. The Spirit arouses and sustains a sense of the faith in the universal body of the faithful, so that its members adhere unfailingly to the faith, penetrate it more deeply, and apply it to life with right judgment; they cannot be mistaken in belief.

The Holy Spirit directs the community of the disciples of Christ on its pilgrimage toward the Father's kingdom. Just as the Spirit of the Lord came upon Christ and anointed him to preach the good news to the poor, so the Spirit sent by Christ from the Father guides the church as it tries to bring Christ's message of salvation to all humankind.

The Holy Spirit continually renews the church and rejuvenates it through the power of the gospel. As it journeys through the temptations and tribulations of this present world, the church continually renews itself under the action of the Holy Spirit, cleansing itself in order to make God present to those around it.

The Holy Spirit is the first installment of our inheritance toward redemption (Eph 1:14). The pilgrim church, with its institutions and sacraments, belongs to this age, which is passing. The end of the ages has reached us. But the church has been sealed with the Spirit as the pledge of things to come, of its future fulfillment. The Spirit points to the future.

These assertions of the influences of the Holy Spirit on the church are from the Second Vatican Council. They are a few of the statements of our beliefs about the Spirit and the church. They lead to the conclusion, the main argument of this book, that the Holy Spirit is the driving force behind the evolution of the church.

The Reign of God and the Church

Jesus of Nazareth proclaimed and preached about the reign of God (or the kingdom of God) all during his public life. It was at the heart of his message. He spoke of it early and often. By comparison, Jesus hardly mentioned the church.

In addition to announcing the reign of God, Jesus actually began it. By his actions he inaugurated it. His miracles of healing and his exorcisms were demonstrations of the power of God coming to the aid of his people through the ministry of Jesus.

The phrase *reign of God* stands for the whole story of God's saving actions, for his powerful rule as king over his people and over his creation. It is a dynamic *happening* involving God, God's people, and all of creation. Jesus spoke of the reign of God as already present in his own time, in his own ministry, and also as in the future, as something yet to come.

At the beginning of his public ministry Jesus said, "Repent, for the kingdom of heaven has come near" (Matt 4:17). Such sayings refer to what is happening at present, in his own ministry. Another instance was in his dialogue with the Pharisees about when the kingdom of God was coming, "For, in fact, the kingdom of God is among you" (Luke 17:21).

Other sayings of Jesus indicate his expectation that the reign of God will come sometime in the future. For example, he taught his disciples to pray, "Your kingdom come" (Matt 6:10) in the Our Father, clearly asking for something that is not yet here.

Another time, near the end of his life, Jesus spoke to his disciples at the last supper, "Truly I tell you, I will never again drink of the fruit of the vine until that day when I drink it new in the kingdom of God" (Mark 14:25). The reign of God was in the future.

No better brief description of the meaning of the reign of God can be found than that in the Preface for the Mass of the Solemnity of Our Lord Jesus Christ, King of the Universe: "an eternal and universal kingdom, a kingdom of truth and life, a kingdom of holiness and grace, a kingdom of justice, love, and peace" (Roman Missal).

After Jesus's departure from this earth, the church assumed his mission and ministry in regard to God's reign. It is not only the message of the church, as it was Jesus's message, but it is the very purpose of the church on earth, its objective, the goal toward which it strives.

Much more than a vaguely distant and uncertain target, the reign of God is a goal of conscious and constant striving for the church. The church is drawn toward it with the power of the Spirit, like a force field that directs its energies. The activities and projects of the church are guided by the Spirit as trajectories toward the values of the kingdom. The reign of God is the evolutionary goal of the people of God, of which the church is a part.

An Overview of the Book

The Holy Spirit is the protagonist of this drama, so Chapter 1 begins with the gradual revelation of the nature and character of the Spirit, beginning with the Old Testament witnesses and then the explicit portrayals of the Spirit in the life, words, and actions of Jesus of Nazareth. The Acts of the Apostles, the letters of Paul, and the other New Testament writings related to the earliest Christian communities complete the divinely revealed portrait of the Spirit.

Chapter 2 traces the post–New Testament period, during which the earliest Christian writers, beginning with the apostolic fathers and the apologists, began to record the experiences of the Spirit in the churches. They were followed by some of the outstanding theological writers of the second to fifth centuries, who reflected on and debated about the nature and actions of the Spirit. This period included the first two ecumenical councils, Nicaea and Constantinople, which gave definitive direction to the church's convictions about the Holy Spirit. The chapter concludes with a summary discussion of the *Filioque* (the Spirit proceeds from the Father *and* the Son) controversy that refused to go away.

The reign of God, explored in Chapter 3, was central to the message of Jesus of Nazareth. He spoke of this mysterious reality all the time, in many different contexts. He referred to it as already begun in his own ministry, and at the same time as still to come, in the future. After Jesus's departure from this earth, the church took over his message and his promotion of the reign of God, the coming in power of God as king over his beloved people and his cherished creation. It is the prime purpose of the church on earth.

The people of God, the chosen people of the Old Testament, was followed by the people of the new covenant, for whom Christ died. This new people of God includes all who follow Christ, all Christians, of whom Catholics are one part, one segment. Here the church encounters its impelling, guiding force, the Holy Spirit, and here, along with the entire people of God, the church proclaims and pursues the reign of God that was announced and begun by Jesus of Nazareth. The Spirit enlivens and directs the church. The reign of God is the goal of the church. This is the focus of Chapter 4.

Turning from the development of the theology of the Holy Spirit, the reign of God and the people of God, to more concrete realities of church structures, Chapter 5 examines the notion of synodality and the ways it can be more effective at every level, the need for diversity and how subsidiary function can enhance it, ministry as it is in the process of being transformed, the selection of bishops and how the process should be modified, and why no more auxiliary bishops should be named.

In Chapter 6 the evolution of three of the church's sacraments is outlined: marriage, from a secular reality to the requirement to be married in canonical form; penance, from public penance in an "order of penitents" to general confession and absolution; and anointing of the sick, from the deathbed to communal celebrations for the sick. There are also suggestions for how they need to be further changed for pastoral reasons.

As a reminder that the church's evolution is an ongoing process rather than a once-and-for-all-time reform, we append an additional set of suggested areas for needed development. The concluding reflection, "Further Directions," includes the areas of the church's teaching function, ecological concerns, and the church's relations with other churches and religions.

Chapter 1

The Evolutionary Force:
The Holy Spirit Revealed in the Bible

The Holy Spirit impels and guides the church and is the driving force behind its evolution. This chapter traces the history of the Spirit's emergence and interventions (1) before the time of Jesus of Nazareth, (2) during the life and ministry of Jesus, and (3) in the formative years of the earliest Christian communities.

The written history of the Holy Spirit begins in the revealed word of God, the Sacred Scriptures, in the Old Testament, with veiled and implicit references. Then in the New Testament come revelations of startling directness in the coming of Jesus Christ, his life, ministry, death, and resurrection. Finally, the Spirit is revealed in the words and actions of Jesus's apostles and disciples, and their successors in the earliest communities of Christians. These are recorded in Acts, the letters, and other writings of the New Testament.

Our perceptions of the Spirit and the Spirit's actions change as new truths are revealed to us. Our understanding and intuitions about the Spirit deepen but are still fragmentary.

Before the Time of Jesus of Nazareth

Pentateuch

The Holy Spirit was revealed to the people of Israel gradually, through the centuries. The Bible traces this revelation beginning with the Genesis creation narratives. The Spirit was described in terms of the powerful presence and creative actions of God, using the images of a mighty wind and the breath of life. "A mighty wind from God swept over the face of the waters" (Gen 1:2) while the earth was depicted as a dark and formless void, on its way to becoming a fruitful earth with seas teeming with creatures.

The second creation narrative reads, "The Lord God formed man from the dust of the ground, and breathed into his nostrils the breath of life; and the man became a living being" (Gen 2:7). This creation myth must be understood within the context of Jewish monotheism; hence, these divine interventions are not yet seen as the actions of a Person within a holy Trinity, but as early manifestations of God's actions in the world.

When Moses instructed the Israelite people on the Lord's commands for the construction and decoration of the sanctuary dwelling, the spirit moved all the members of the community to contribute. "Then all the congregation of the Israelites withdrew from the presence of Moses. And they came, everyone whose heart was stirred, and everyone whose spirit was willing, and brought the Lord's offering to be used for the tent of meeting and for all its service, and for all the sacred vestments" (Exod 35:20–21). The spirit prompted the hearts of the members of the community to give materials and skills to construct a dwelling for the Lord.

In the book of Numbers we find a fascinating sharing of the spirit by the seventy elders of Israel during their exodus journey. Moses complained to the Lord about the burden of people's discontent, and the Lord gave him seventy inspired assistants.

> So the Lord said to Moses, "Gather for me seventy of the elders of Israel, whom you know to be the elders of the people and officers over them; bring them to the tent of meeting, and have them take their place there with you. I will come down and talk with you there; and I will take some of the spirit that is on you, and put it on them; and they shall bear the burden of the people along with you so that you will not bear it all by yourself."
>
> So Moses went out and told the people the words of the Lord; and he gathered seventy elders of the people,

and placed them all around the tent. Then the Lord came down in the cloud and spoke to him, and took some of the spirit that was on him and put it on the seventy elders; and when the spirit rested upon them, they prophesied. (Num 11:16–17, 24–25)

Psalms

The creative imagery for the spirit found in Genesis is echoed in the book of Psalms. The creatures of the earth look to God to give them food in due time. "When you take away their breath they die and return to their dust. When you send forth your spirit they are created; and you renew the face of the ground" (Ps 104:29–30). In one of the penitential psalms the spirit is envisioned as part of the deliverance from sin, and is called "holy." "Create in me a clean heart, O God, and put a new and steadfast spirit within me. Do not cast me away from your presence, and do not take your holy spirit from me. Restore to me the joy of your salvation, and sustain in me a willing spirit" (Ps 51:10–12).

The spirit is pervasive; it is everywhere.

"O Lord, you have searched me and known me. You know when I sit down and rise up; you discern my thoughts from far away. . . . Where can I go from your spirit? Or where can I flee from your presence? If I ascend to heaven, you are there; if I make my bed in Sheol, you are there." (Ps 139:1, 7)

The spirit of God aroused Israel's leaders to take action in defense of their people. "The spirit of the Lord took possession of Gideon; and he sounded the trumpet, and the Abiezrites were called out to follow him" (Judg 6:34). The exploits of Samson, son of Manoah, were framed with interventions of the spirit. "The woman bore a son, and named him Samson. The boy grew and the Lord blessed him. The spirit of the Lord began to stir him" (Judg 13:24–25). Later, before each of his violent triumphs—the encounter with the young lion, the killing of the thirty men of Ashkelon, the victory over a thousand Philistines—the scripture said: "The spirit of the Lord rushed upon him" (Judg 14:6, 19; 15:14).

In the time of Israel's kings, we read: "As Saul turned away to leave Samuel, God gave him another heart. . . . When they were going from there to Gibeah, a band of prophets met him; and the spirit of God possessed him, and he fell into a prophetic frenzy with them" (1 Sam 10:9–10). "The spirit of God came upon Saul in power . . . and his anger was greatly kindled" (1 Sam 11:6). The judge Samuel was sent by the Lord to anoint David, the youngest of Jesse's sons, as the king of Israel. When David arrived "The Lord said, 'Rise and anoint him; for this is the one.' Then Samuel took the horn of oil, and anointed him in the presence of his brothers; and the spirit of the Lord came mightily upon David from that day forward" (1 Sam 16:12–13). Later, when Saul was in pursuit of David, "The spirit of God came upon Saul. As he was going he fell into a prophetic frenzy" (1 Sam 19:23). We might describe these interventions as personal inspirations, but they clearly give us a sense of the ways in which God directed his chosen people.

Prophets

The prophet Isaiah described the dimensions of the spirit as a part of the Immanuel prophecy. "A shoot shall come out from the stock of Jesse [David's father] and a branch shall grow out of his roots. The spirit of the Lord shall rest on him: the spirit of wisdom and understanding, the spirit of counsel and might, the spirit of knowledge and the fear of the Lord" (Isa 11:1–2). The prophet Micah contrasted the authenticity of his own message with the false prophets of his day by emphasizing his possession of God's spirit: "But as for me, I am filled with power, with the spirit of the Lord, and with justice and might, to declare to Jacob his transgression and to Israel his sin" (Mic 3:8).

Ezekiel described his own calling by the Lord in terms of receiving the spirit. "He said to me: O mortal, stand up on your feet, and I will speak with you. And when he spoke to me, a spirit entered into me and set me on my feet; and I heard him speaking to me" (Ezek 2:2). And again, "The spirit lifted me up and brought me to the east gate of the house of the Lord, which faces east. . . . Then the spirit of the Lord fell upon me, and he said to me, 'Say, thus says the Lord: This is what you think, O

house of Israel; I know the things that come into your mind'"
(Ezek 11:1, 5).

Ezekiel spoke of the Lord's regeneration of the house of Israel
in terms of a new heart and a new spirit:

> A new heart I will give you, and a new spirit I will put
> within you; and I will remove from your body the heart
> of stone and give you a heart of flesh. I will put my spirit
> within you, and make you follow my statutes, and be care-
> ful to observe my ordinances. Then you shall live in the
> land that I gave to your ancestors; and you shall be my
> people and I shall be your God. (Ezek 36:26–28)

The prophet Ezekiel presented the most vivid picture of the
enlivening power of the spirit in his famous vision of the dry
bones. The vision prophesied the regeneration of the people of
Israel after their exile in Babylon. This spectacular vision brought
together the images of wind and breath in the restoration of the
people to new life.

> The hand of the Lord came upon me, and he brought me
> out by the spirit of the Lord and set me down in the middle
> of a valley; it was full of bones. He led me all round them;
> there were very many lying in the valley, and they were
> very dry. He said to me, "Mortal, can these bones live?" I
> answered, "O Lord God, you know." Then he said to me,
> "Prophesy to these bones and say to them: O dry bones,
> hear the word of the Lord. Thus says the Lord God to these
> bones: I will cause breath to enter you, and you shall live. I
> will lay sinews on you, and will cause flesh to come upon
> you, and cover you with skin, and put breath in you, and
> you shall live; and you shall know that I am the Lord."
> So I prophesied as I had been commanded; and as I
> prophesied, suddenly there was a noise, a rattling, and the
> bones came together, bone to its bone. I looked and there
> were sinews on them, and flesh had come upon them, and
> skin had covered them; but there was no breath in them.
> Then he said to me, "Prophesy to the breath, mortal, and
> say to the breath: Thus says the Lord God: Come from the
> four winds, O breath, and breathe upon these slain that

they might live." I prophesied as he commanded me, and the breath came into them, and they lived, and stood on their feet, a vast multitude.

Then he said to me, "Mortal, these bones are the whole house of Israel." (Ezek 37:1–11)

Ezekiel celebrated the return and restoration of Israel with words of the spirit outpoured.

Then they shall know that I am the Lord their God because I sent them into exile among the nations, and then gathered them into their own land. I will leave none of them behind, and I will never again hide my face from them, when I pour out my spirit upon the house of Israel, says the Lord God. (Ezek 39:28–29)

In Second Isaiah the prophet featured the role of the spirit in the first of his "Servant of the Lord" songs, oracles whose fulfillment Christians later attributed to Jesus Christ.

Here is my servant, whom I uphold, my chosen, in whom my soul delights; I have put my spirit upon him; he will bring forth justice to the nations.

Thus says God the Lord, who created the heavens and stretched them out, who spread out the earth and what comes from it, who gives breath to the people upon it and spirit to those who walk in it. (Isa 42:1, 5)

Isaiah spoke of the restoration of Israel as an outpouring of the spirit of the Lord. "I will pour my spirit upon your descendants, and my blessing on your offspring" (Isa 44:3).

In Third Isaiah the prophet wrote about the spirit's part in restoration of Israel after the exile.

The spirit of the Lord God is upon me, because the Lord has anointed me; he has sent me to bring good news to the oppressed, to bind up the broken-hearted, to proclaim liberty to the captives, and release to the prisoners; to proclaim the year of the Lord's favor. (Isa 61:1–2)

Jesus quoted this passage from Isaiah in reference to his own mission when speaking in the synagogue at Nazareth at the beginning of his public ministry (Luke 4:18–19).

Again in Third Isaiah the spirit was described as involved in the deliverance of Israel:

> But they rebelled [against the Lord] and grieved his holy spirit; therefore he became their enemy; he himself fought against them. Then they remembered the days of old: of Moses and his servant. Where is the one who brought them up out of the sea with the shepherds of his flock? Where is the one who put within them his holy spirit . . . ? Like cattle that go down into the valley, the spirit of the Lord gave them rest. (Isa 63:10–11, 14)

Here, for the second time, the spirit of the Lord is called holy.

The prophet Joel spoke of the Lord's deliverance of his people, a blessed time of peace and prosperity after a terrible invasion of locusts when the Lord will send his spirit on all of his people.

> I will pour out my spirit on all flesh; your sons and your daughters shall prophesy, your old men shall dream dreams, and your young men shall see visions. Even on the male and female slaves, in those days, I will pour out my spirit. (Joel 2:28–29)

The apostle Peter quoted Joel's words at the Pentecost event, to the effect that the Holy Spirit was given to Jesus's disciples in fulfillment of Joel's prophecy (Acts 2:14–21).

The prophet Micah defended his own authentic role against the false prophets who led the people astray by asserting his possession of the spirit: "But as for me, I am filled with power, with the spirit of the Lord, and with justice and might, to declare to Jacob his transgressions and to Israel his sins" (Mic 3:9). Micah claimed that the spirit was the source of his moral authority.

Wisdom

The Old Testament vision of the spirit came into clearer focus in the Wisdom literature. In the book of Job, for instance, the spirit was seen as the source of wisdom. "But truly it is the spirit in a mortal, the breath of the Almighty, that makes for understanding" (Job 32:8).

The book of Wisdom, written about a hundred years before Christ, when speaking about holy wisdom, gave this description of the spirit of the Lord that knows all things:

> For wisdom is a kindly spirit, but will not free blasphemers from the guilt of their words; because God is witness of their inmost feelings, and a true observer of their hearts, and a hearer of their tongues. Because the spirit of the Lord has filled the world, and that which holds all things together knows what is said, therefore those who utter unrighteous things will not escape notice, and justice, when it punishes, will not pass them by. (Wis 1:6–8)

> I called on God, and the spirit of wisdom came to me. . . . There is in her a spirit that is intelligent, holy, unique, manifold, subtle, mobile, clear, unpolluted, distinct, invulnerable, loving the good, keen, irresistible, beneficent, humane, steadfast, sure, free from anxiety, all-powerful, overseeing all, and penetrating through all spirits that are intelligent, pure, and altogether subtle. . . . For she is a breath of the power of God, and a pure emanation of the glory of the Almighty . . . for she is a reflection of eternal light, a spotless mirror of the working of God, and an image of his goodness. (Wis 7:7, 22–23, 25–26)

Summary

Thus was the Spirit gradually revealed to the people of Israel (and to us) in the Old Testament. Not all at once, but over the course of several centuries and through the writings of many authors. Not in a clear and concise theological treatise, but in images of wind and breath and spirit, in allusions to the actions of the Lord God, in the process of creation, in the messages sent through the prophets, in key moments in the history and renewal of the chosen people, in the prayers and praise of temple worship, and in the increasingly personal language of holy wisdom.

These many and diverse references to the spirit of God form a complex mosaic that reveals a profile of the Holy Spirit. A picture of the Holy Spirit with more depth and greater clarity was painted by Jesus of Nazareth. His life and words made explicit what was implicit the powerful Old Testament imagery of the Spirit.

The Life and Ministry of Jesus of Nazareth

The revelation of the nature and working of the Holy Spirit is made more explicit in the New Testament, beginning with the action of the Spirit in the very act of the incarnation of Christ.

Annunciation and Birth

The Holy Spirit enters the story of Jesus of Nazareth before his birth, even before his conception. The encounter between the angel Gabriel and Mary took place in the town of Nazareth in Galilee. It was her affirmative response to Gabriel's message that made her conception of Jesus possible.

> The angel said to her, "Do not be afraid, Mary, for you have found favor with God. And now, you will conceive in your womb and bear a son and you shall name him Jesus. He will be great, and will be called the Son of the Most High, and the Lord God will give him the throne of his ancestor David. He will reign over the house of Jacob forever, and of his kingdom there will be no end." Mary said to the angel, "How can this be, since I am a virgin?" The angel said to her, "The Holy Spirit will come upon you, and the power of the Most High will overshadow you; therefore the child to be born will be holy, he will be called Son of God." . . . Then Mary said, "Here am I, the servant of the Lord; let it be with me according to your word." (Luke 1:30–35, 38)

The role of the Holy Spirit in the conception of Jesus was reaffirmed in Matthew's version of the events:

Now the birth of Jesus the Messiah took place in this way. When his mother Mary had been engaged to Joseph, but before they had lived together, she was found to be with child from the Holy Spirit. Her husband Joseph . . . planned to dismiss her quietly. But just when he had resolved to do this, an angel of the Lord appeared to him in a dream and said, "Joseph, son of David, do not be afraid to take Mary as your wife, for the child conceived in her is from the Holy Spirit. She will bear a son, and you are to name him Jesus, for he will save his people from their sins." (Matt 1:18–21)

The incarnation of the Son of God took place through the willing cooperation of God's Holy Spirit and the Jewish maid of Nazareth. The Spirit, the giver of life, entered our world in order to enable the birth of Jesus the Christ, with Mary's welcoming acceptance of God's initiative. Her acceptance showed a new level of cooperation between the human and the divine.

Shortly after the birth of Jesus in the town of Bethlehem in Judea, his parents took him up to the temple in Jerusalem to present him to the Lord. There they encountered a devout man named Simeon, who was much influenced by the Holy Spirit. Luke mentions the Spirit three times in recounting this encounter with Simeon:

Now there was a man in Jerusalem named Simeon; this man was righteous and devout, looking forward to the consolation of Israel, the Holy Spirit rested on him. It had been revealed to him by the Holy Spirit that he would not see death before he had seen the Lord's Messiah. Guided by the Spirit, Simeon came into the temple, and when the parents brought in the child Jesus, to do for him what was customary under the law, Simeon took him into his arms and praised God saying, "Master, now you are dismissing your servant in peace, according to your word; for my eyes have seen your salvation, which you have prepared in the presence of all peoples, a light for revelation to the Gentiles, and for glory to your people Israel." (Luke 2:25–32)

Speaking through Simeon, the Holy Spirit proclaimed the salvific mission of Jesus, the long-awaited Messiah, even while he was an infant in arms.

The Baptism of Jesus

The baptism of the adult Jesus in the Jordan River by John the Baptist was framed, described, and detailed as a Spirit event. It predicted and portrayed the ministry of Jesus as a work of the Holy Spirit. First the prediction:

> [John] went into all the region around the Jordan, proclaiming a baptism of repentance for the forgiveness of sins, as it is written in the book of the words of the prophet Isaiah, "The voice of one crying out in the wilderness: Prepare the way of the Lord, make his paths straight. . . . All flesh shall see the salvation of God." . . .
>
> "I baptize you with water; but one who is more powerful than I is coming; I am not worthy to untie the thong of his sandals. He will baptize you with the Holy Spirit and with fire."
>
> Now when all the people were baptized, and when Jesus also had been baptized and was praying, the heaven was opened, and the Holy Spirit descended upon him in bodily form like a dove. And a voice came from heaven, "You are my Son, the Beloved; with you I am well pleased." (Luke 3:3–4, 6, 16, 21–22)

The Gospel according to Mark, in the very first chapter, describes these events in almost exactly the same words (Mark 1:2–11). Matthew's Gospel repeats nearly the same words in a slightly different order (Matt 3:11–17).

The realization of the baptism "with the Holy Spirit" that Jesus was to bring was in fulfillment of the messianic prophecies of Isaiah (44:3), Ezekiel (39:29), and Joel (2:28). His mission of salvation was also the work of the Spirit; the beloved Son and the Holy Spirit acted together in dynamic collaboration.

Temptation of Jesus

After his baptism in the Jordan and after the heavenly voice proclaimed, "You are my son, the Beloved; in you I am well pleased," the next verse states: "And the Spirit immediately drove him out into the wilderness. He was in the wilderness for forty days, tempted by Satan; and he was with the wild beasts; and the angels waited on him" (Mark 1:11–13). "Jesus, full of the Holy Spirit, returned from the Jordan and was led by the Spirit in the wilderness, where for forty days he was tempted by the devil" (Luke 4:1–2).

Matthew and Luke narrate the three temptations of Jesus by the devil in colorful detail: (1) Jesus was famished after fasting for forty days, the devil suggested that he turn the stones into loaves of bread; (2) the devil took him up a high mountain where he could see all the kingdoms of the world, and he offered them to Jesus if he would worship him; and (3) the devil took Jesus to the pinnacle of the temple in Jerusalem and told him that if he was the Son of God to throw himself down and God would save him. Jesus did not succumb to any of the devil's temptations (Luke 4:2–12). "When the devil had finished every test, he departed from him until an opportune time" (Luke 4:13). Jesus's contest with the powers of darkness was far from finished.

Public Ministry

The very next verse in Luke's Gospel is, "Then Jesus, filled with the power of the Spirit, returned to Galilee, and a report about him spread through all the surrounding country. He began to teach in their synagogues and was praised by everyone" (Luke 4:14–15). His Spirit-supported ministry moved from personal to public.

Luke illustrates this entry of Jesus into the public sphere by narrating the scene in the Nazareth synagogue, immediately after the "filled with the power of the Spirit" description:

When [Jesus] came to Nazareth, where he had been brought up, he went to the synagogue on the sabbath day, as was his custom. He stood up to read, and the scroll of the prophet Isaiah was given to him. He unrolled the scroll and found the place where it was written: "The Spirit of the Lord is upon me, because he has anointed me to bring glad tidings to the poor. He has sent me to proclaim release to the captives and recovery of sight to the blind, to let the oppressed go free, and to proclaim the year of the Lord's favor." And he rolled up the scroll, gave it back to the attendant and sat down. The eyes of all in the synagogue were fixed on him. Then he began to say to them, "Today this scripture has been fulfilled in your hearing." (Luke 4:16–21)

Jesus identified himself as the "anointed one" upon whom "the Spirit of the Lord" rested, the Messiah who had come to fulfill Isaiah's prophecy of good news for the oppressed and brokenhearted, freedom for captives and prisoners. This theme of Jesus's concern for the poor, downtrodden, and neglected is a characteristic of Luke's Gospel. "All spoke well of him and were amazed at the gracious words that came from his mouth" (Luke 4:23).

The Spirit was present and active in Jesus's ministry of preaching and healing. In his dispute with the Pharisees who accused him of casting out demons by the power of the prince of demons, Jesus stated: "But if it is by the Spirit of God that I cast out demons, then the kingdom of God has come to you. . . . Whoever speaks against the Holy Spirit will not be forgiven" (Matt 12:28, 32; Luke 12:10).

When he sent out his disciples on their mission, Jesus equipped them with the power from the Spirit: "Then Jesus summoned his twelve disciples and gave them authority over unclean spirits, to cast them out, and to cure every disease and every sickness" (Matt 10:1). He warned them that they would be misunderstood and even persecuted. But they should not be worried about how to defend themselves. "When they hand you over, do not worry about how you are to speak or what you are to say; for what you are to say will be given to you at that time; for it is not you who speak, but the Spirit of your Father speaking through you" (Matt 10:20; Luke 12:12).

The evangelist Luke speaks of a second missionary sending by Jesus. Upon the return of the seventy-two disciples, they said:

> "Lord, in your name even the demons submit to us!" . . . At that same hour Jesus rejoiced in the Holy Spirit and said, "I thank you, Father, Lord of heaven and earth, because you have hidden these things from the wise and the intelligent, and revealed them to infants; yes, Father, for such was your gracious will." (Luke 10:17, 21)

Matthew portrays Jesus as fulfilling the first of the Servant Songs of the prophet Isaiah, after Jesus had cured many who were ill: "Here is my servant, whom I have chosen, my beloved, with whom my soul is well pleased. I will put my Spirit upon him, and he will proclaim justice to the Gentiles" (Matt 12:18). The prophecy points to Jesus, guided by the Spirit, reaching out from Israel to all nations.

When Jesus was teaching his disciples how to pray, he told them,

> "Ask and it will be given to you; search, and you will find; knock, and the door will be opened for you. . . . Is there anyone among you who, if your child asks for a fish, will give a snake instead of a fish? . . . If you then, who are evil, know how to give good gifts to your children, how much more will the heavenly Father give the Holy Spirit to those who ask him." (Luke 11:9, 11, 13)

The gift of the Holy Spirit was viewed as the answer to the prayer of the Christian disciple.

In his final commission to his disciples, Jesus said to them, "All authority on heaven and on earth has been given to me. Go therefore and make disciples of all nations, baptizing them in the name of the Father and of the Son and of the Holy Spirit, and teaching them to obey everything that I have commanded you" (Matt 28:19–20). This trinitarian formula may have been quoted from the baptismal rite used in Matthew's community; it demonstrates that the Holy Spirit was integral to Christ's core message, alongside his own relationship to the Father.

The Gospel of John

John's Gospel was composed later than the other Gospels and reflects a different and distinctive vision of Jesus, as the Word of God and Son of God, present at creation.

> In the beginning was the Word, and the Word was with God, and the Word was God. . . . All things came into being through him, and without him not one thing came into being.
> And the Word became flesh and lived among us, and we have seen his glory, the glory as of a father's only son, full of grace and truth. (John 1:1, 3, 14)

A man named John, whom we know as John the Baptist, was sent by God to give testimony to Jesus. When he was questioned as he baptized in Bethany across the Jordan, he asserted that he was not the Messiah or one of the prophets.

> The next day he saw Jesus coming towards him, and declared, "Here is the Lamb of God who takes away the sin of the world! This is he of whom I said, 'After me comes a man who ranks ahead of me because he was before me.' I myself did not know him; but I came baptizing with water for this reason, that he might be revealed to Israel."
> And John testified, "I saw the Spirit descending from heaven like a dove, and it remained on him. I myself did not know him, but the one who sent me to baptize with water said to me, 'He on whom you see the Spirit descend and remain is the one who baptizes with the Holy Spirit.' And I myself have seen and have testified that this is the Son of God." (John 1:29–34)

Jesus was identified as the permanent bearer of the Spirit, the one with whom the Spirit remains or abides, the one who baptizes with the Holy Spirit, and the one who "gives the Spirit without measure" (John 3:34).

Jesus told Nicodemus, one of the rulers of the Jews who realized that Jesus was a teacher who had come from God, and who came at night to question him, that "no one can enter the kingdom of God without being born of water and Spirit" (John 3:5). The Spirit causes a new beginning, a regeneration, a rebirth, a renewal.

In his encounter with the Samaritan woman at the well, Jesus spoke of giving her "living water":

> "Those who drink of the water that I will give them will never be thirsty. The water that I will give will become in them a spring of water gushing up to eternal life. . . . The hour is coming and is now here, when the true worshipers will worship the Father in spirit and in truth, for the Father seeks such as these to worship him. God is spirit and those who worship him must worship in spirit and truth." (John 3:14, 23–24)

The Spirit of God purifies the believer and is a permanent endowment.

Jesus proclaimed that those who believed in him would become the source of "living water," the re-vivifying Spirit:

> On the last day of the festival [of Tabernacles], the great day, while Jesus was standing there, he cried out, "Let anyone who is thirsty, come to me, and let the one who believes in me drink. As the scripture has said, 'Out of the believer's heart shall flow rivers of living water.'" Now he said this about the Spirit, which believers in him were to receive. (John 7:37–39)

In the Gospel of John, the Spirit would only be fully given to Christ's disciples after his death and resurrection (John 7:39; 20:22).

Another Advocate

John's Gospel devotes a long section (four chapters) to Jesus's farewell discourse with his disciples at the last supper, just before his arrest, trial, and crucifixion. In this discourse Jesus told his disciples of "another advocate" whom the Father would send to be with them to guide and assist them, after his own departure.

It was the promise of the Holy Spirit in a new role and with a new title.

> "If you love me, you will keep my commandments. And I will ask the Father, and he will give you another Advocate, and he will be with you for ever. This is the Spirit of truth, whom the world cannot receive because it neither sees him or knows him. You know him because he abides with you, and he will be in you." (John 14:15–17)

> "I have said these things to you while I am still with you. But the Advocate, the Holy Spirit, whom the Father will send in my name, will teach you everything, and remind you of all I have said to you." (John 14:25–26)

> "When the Advocate comes, whom I will send you from the Father, the Spirit of truth who comes from the Father, he will testify on my behalf." (John 15:26)

> "I tell you the truth: it is to your advantage that I go away, for if I do not go away, the Advocate will not come to you; but if I go I will send him to you." (John 16:7)

> "I still have many things to say to you, but you cannot bear them now. When the Spirit of truth comes, he will guide you into all the truth; for he will not speak on his own, but will speak whatever he hears, and he will declare to you the things that are to come. He will glorify me, because he will take what is mine and declare it to you. All that the Father has is mine. For this reason I said he will take what is mine and declare it to you." (John 16: 12–15)

The name *advocate* or *paraclete* means a consoler, comforter, or helper. The Spirit's role under this name is to be with the disciples to guide and teach them. He is to serve as a teacher within them who will guide the followers of Christ to the truth, the same truth that the Father entrusted to Christ. The future was unknown, but they had the Holy Spirit as their guide.

The final and formal conferral of the Holy Spirit on Jesus's disciples took place on the evening of the first day of the week after his crucifixion, when the risen Lord stood among them and said:

> "Peace be with you. As the Father has sent me, so I send you." When he had said this he breathed on them and said to them, "Receive the Holy Spirit. If you forgive the sins of any, they are forgiven them; if you retain the sins of any, they are retained." (John 20:22)

The breath of the risen Christ conveyed the Holy Spirit to the disciples and to those who gathered with them and followed after them in the church, a community of forgiveness.

Summary

The stories about the life and ministry of Jesus of Nazareth, called Gospels, tell us vastly more about the Holy Spirit than we are able to glean from the Old Testament. They reveal a more profound understanding of the Spirit.

Present even before Jesus was conceived in Mary's womb, the overshadowing Spirit, with Mary's willing consent, caused the incarnation of the Son, thus initiating Jesus's mission of our salvation. That same Spirit descended on Jesus at his baptism in the bodily form of a dove and remained with him. The Holy Spirit "filled" Jesus for his forty days of temptations by the devil in the wilderness and "filled" him with power at the outset of his public ministry. Jesus cast out demons by the Spirit of God. He said that the Father will give the Holy Spirit to those who ask him. Jesus commanded his disciples to go forth and baptize in the name of the Father and of the Son and of the Holy Spirit. Jesus said that those who believed in him would receive the Spirit when they came to him to drink of the "living water" he offered to the thirsty. Jesus promised that the Father would send "another advocate" to his followers after he left them, the Spirit of Truth, who would guide them to all truth. The risen Lord breathed on his disciples at the last and gave them the Holy Spirit for the forgiveness of sins. He promised them that they would be baptized with the Spirit and receive power when the Holy Spirit came upon them.

In the Formative Years of the Earliest Christian Communities

In addition to the Gospel that bears his name, Luke wrote the Acts of the Apostles, which chronicles the founding and development of early Christian communities after Jesus was taken up to heaven. Luke links the two volumes with references to the sending of the Holy Spirit, "the promise of the Father." At the end of the gospel narrative, Jesus said to his disciples:

> "Thus it is written that the Messiah is to suffer and to rise from the dead on the third day, and that repentance and forgiveness of sins is to be proclaimed in his name to all nations, beginning from Jerusalem. You are witnesses of these things. And see, I am sending upon you what my Father promised; so stay here in the city until you have been clothed with power from on high." (Luke 24:46–49)

At the very beginning of the Acts of the Apostles, the same author writes:

> In the first book, Theophilus, I wrote about all that Jesus did and taught from the beginning until the day he was taken up to heaven, after giving instruction through the Holy Spirit to the apostles whom he had chosen. . . . While staying with them, he ordered them not to leave Jerusalem, but to wait there for the promise of the Father. "This," he said, "is what you have heard from me; for John baptized with water, but you will be baptized with the Holy Spirit not many days from now." (Acts 1:1–2, 4–5)

As Jesus prepared to depart from his disciples, he said to them, "You will receive power when the Holy Spirit has come upon you, and you will be my witnesses in Jerusalem, in all Judea and Samaria, and to the ends of the earth" (Acts 1:8). He prepared his followers to receive the Spirit as he had; the Spirit would be poured out upon and reside within those who believed in Jesus, just as the Spirit had rested upon and acted with Jesus himself. Their witness to him, empowered by the Spirit, would move from Israel to the ends of the earth.

The Pentecost Event

Fifty days after the Passover celebration came the feast of Pentecost (Lev 23:15–16; Tob 2:1), and on that day the Holy Spirit was poured out upon the disciples of Jesus, as he had promised.

> When the day of Pentecost had come, they were all together in one place, and suddenly from heaven there came a sound like the rush of a violent wind, and it filled the entire house where they were sitting. Divided tongues, as of fire, appeared among them, and a tongue rested on each of them. All of them were filled with the Holy Spirit and began to speak in other languages, as the Spirit gave them ability. (Acts 2:1–4)

The symbols that accompanied this dramatic conferral of the Holy Spirit had powerful resonance with earlier events: the mighty wind from God that swept over the face of the waters in the first creation story (Gen 1:2), and the Lord's descent in fire on Mount Sinai for the giving of the commandments and the covenant (Exod 19:18; 24:17). The source of the sound like the rush of a violent wind was heaven, indicating God as its origin. The division of the tongues of fire showed that the Spirit was destined for each member of the assembly. This outpouring of the Spirit accompanied by tongues of fire was the fulfillment of John the Baptist's prediction: "I baptize you with water, but one who is more powerful than I is coming. . . . He will baptize you with the Holy Spirit and with fire" (Luke 3:16; Matt 3:11).

The Spirit-given ability "to speak in other languages" about "God's deeds of power" may have been the opening indicator of the apostolic mission that would cross all language boundaries.

The apostle Peter spoke right after the Pentecost event. He explained that what had just taken place was "what was spoken through the prophet Joel":

In the last days it will be, God declares, that I will pour out my Spirit upon all flesh, and your sons and daughters shall prophesy, and your young men shall see visions, and your old men shall dream dreams. Even upon my slaves, both men and women, in those days I will pour out my Spirit and they shall prophesy. (Acts 2:17–18)

Peter went on to proclaim,

You that are Israelites, listen to what I have to say: Jesus of Nazareth, a man attested to you by God with deeds of power, wonders, and signs that God did through him among you, as you yourselves know—this man, handed over to you according to the definite plan and foreknowledge of God, you crucified and killed by the hands of those outside the law. But God raised him up, having freed him from death, because it was impossible for him to be held in its power. . . . This Jesus God raised up, and of that all of us are witnesses. Being therefore exalted at the right hand of God, and having received from the Father the promise of the Holy Spirit, he has poured out this that you see and hear. . . . Therefore, let the entire house of Israel know with certainty that God has made him both Lord and Messiah, this Jesus whom you crucified. (Acts 2:22–24, 32–33, 36)

Peter's hearers were "cut to the heart" at these words, and they asked Peter and the other apostles what they should do.

Peter said to them, "Repent, and be baptized every one of you in the name of Jesus Christ so that your sins may be forgiven; and you will receive the gift of the Holy Spirit. For the promise is for you, for your children, and for all who are far away, everyone whom the Lord our God calls to him." . . . So those who welcomed his message were baptized, and that day about three thousand persons were added. (Acts 2:38–39, 41)

The Community in Jerusalem

Sometime later Peter and John were on their way to the temple to pray, and they encountered a man who had been crippled from birth begging for alms at the temple gate.

> Peter looked intently at him, as did John, and said, "Look at us." And he fixed his attention on them, expecting to receive something from them. But Peter said, "I have no silver or gold, but what I have I give you, in the name of Jesus of Nazareth, stand up and walk." And he took him by the right hand and raised him up; and immediately his feet and ankles were made strong. Jumping up, he stood and began to walk, and he entered the temple with them, walking and leaping, and praising God. (Acts 3:4–8)

The people who saw this event recognized the crippled man who used to beg for alms, and they were filled with wonder and amazement at what had happened to him. They gathered around Peter and John and the man made strong, and Peter explained to them that it was through the name of Jesus that he was healed:

> And by faith in his name, his name itself has made this man strong, whom you see and know, and the faith that is through Jesus has given him this perfect health in the presence of all of you. (Acts 3:16)

The temple authorities came and arrested Peter and John "because they were teaching the people and proclaiming that in Jesus there is resurrection from the dead" (Acts 4:2) and put them in custody to be tried before the Sanhedrin. Peter and John defended themselves vigorously (Peter was "filled with the Holy Spirit"—Acts 4:8), and the man who had been cured stood beside them. The Sanhedrin could find no way to punish them because the people knew and praised God for what had happened.

After they were released, they went to their friends and reported what the chief priests and elders had said to them. When they heard it, they raised their voices together to God:

"For in this city, in fact, both Herod and Pontius Pilate, with the Gentiles and the peoples of Israel, gathered together against your holy servant Jesus, whom you anointed to do whatever your hand and your plan had predestined to take place. And now, Lord, look at their threats, and grant to your servants to speak your word with all boldness, while you stretch out your hand to heal, and signs and wonders are performed through the name of your holy servant Jesus." When they had prayed, the place in which they were gathered together was shaken; and they were all filled with the Holy Spirit and spoke the word of God with boldness. (Acts 4:27–31)

The young community of the followers of Jesus in Jerusalem began to grow, despite the suspicions of the Jewish authorities. Their consciousness of the Holy Spirit within them encouraged them to speak the word of God with boldness.

Now many signs and wonders were done among the people by the apostles . . . so that they even carried out the sick into the streets, and laid them on cots and mats, in order that Peter's shadow might fall on some of them as he came by. A great number of people would also gather from the towns around Jerusalem, bringing the sick and those tormented by unclean spirits, and they were all cured. (Acts 5:12, 15–16)

The high priest and the Sadducees laid hands on the apostles and put them in jail. But, during the night an angel of the Lord opened the doors of the prison and told them to go into the temple area and tell the people all about this life. In the morning, when the Sanhedrin—the full senate of the Israelites—was convened, it sent to the jail for the apostles only to discover that they were in the temple area teaching the people. The authorities had them brought in, but without using force, for fear of being stoned by the people.

When they had brought them, they had them stand before the council. The high priest questioned them, saying, "We gave you strict orders not to teach in this name, yet here you have filled Jerusalem with your teaching and you are determined to bring this man's blood on us." But Peter and the apostles answered, "We must obey God rather than any human authority. The God of our ancestors raised up Jesus, whom you had killed by hanging him on a tree. God exalted him at his right hand as Leader and Savior, so that he might give repentance to Israel and forgiveness of sins. And we are witnesses to these things, and so is the Holy Spirit whom God has given to those who obey him." (Acts 5:27–32)

The members of the council were enraged at these words, and wanted to kill the apostles, but one of the council, a Pharisee named Gamaliel, warned the others that they might find themselves in opposition to God:

"So in the present case, I tell you, keep away from these men and let them alone; because if this plan or this undertaking is of human origin, it will fail; but if it is of God, you will not be able to overthrow them—in that case you may even be found fighting against God!" (Acts 5:38–39)

The Sanhedrin was convinced by Gamaliel, so they had the apostles flogged, ordered them not to speak in the name of Jesus, and let them go.

As they left the council the apostles rejoiced that they were considered worthy to suffer dishonor for the sake of the name. And every day in the temple and at home they did not cease to teach and proclaim Jesus as the Messiah. (Acts 5:41–42)

Even as official opposition to them increased, the Jerusalem community continued to give testimony to Jesus as the Holy Spirit led them to do.

Stephen's Selection, Trial, and Death

The story of Stephen reveals an early tension within the Jerusalem community between the native Hebrew speakers and those Jews returned from the diaspora who spoke only Greek.

The community, under the direction of the apostles, elected seven men, all with Greek names, to a role of service to the needy among its Greek-speaking members. Stephen was the first named among them, and he was described as "a man filled with faith and the Holy Spirit" (Acts 6:5).

Stephen was soon seen as "filled with grace and power, working great wonders and signs among the people," and those who debated with him "could not withstand the wisdom and spirit with which he spoke" (Acts 6:8, 10). His opponents accused Stephen of blasphemy and had him brought before the Sanhedrin. Their witnesses said, "This man never stops saying things against this holy place and the law, for we have heard him say that this Jesus of Nazareth will destroy this place, and will change the customs that Moses handed on to us" (Acts 6:13–15).

Stephen launched into a long discourse in his own defense, citing many times in the past when Israel's people were unfaithful to God's designs. (This narrative was Luke's way of indicating the separation of Christianity from its Jewish roots.) Stephen ended his discourse before the Sanhedrin this way:

> "You stiff-necked people, uncircumcised in heart and ears, you are forever opposing the Holy Spirit, just as your ancestors used to do. Which of the prophets did your ancestors not persecute? They killed those who foretold the coming of the Righteous One, and now you have become his betrayers and murderers. You are the ones that received the law as ordained by angels, and yet you have not kept it."
>
> When they heard these things, they became enraged and ground their teeth at Stephen. But filled with the Holy Spirit, he gazed into heaven and saw the glory of God and Jesus standing at the right hand of God. "Look," he said, "I see the heavens opened and the Son of Man standing at the right hand of God!" But they covered their ears, and with a loud shout all rushed together against him. They dragged him out of the city and began to stone him . . . While they were stoning Stephen, he prayed, "Lord Jesus, receive my spirit." Then he knelt down and cried out in a loud voice, "Lord, do not hold this sin against them." When he had said this, he died. . . .

> That day a severe persecution began against the church in Jerusalem, and all except the apostles were scattered throughout the countryside of Judea and Samaria. (Acts 7:51–60; 8:1)

Thus began the spread of the word about Jesus the Messiah outside of Jerusalem and into towns to the north and south, in the regions of Samaria and Judea.

The Samaria Community

Philip, one of the seven Greek-speakers chosen by the Jerusalem community along with Stephen, went to the city of Samaria to proclaim the Messiah.

> The crowds with one accord listened eagerly to what was said by Philip, hearing and seeing the signs that he did, for unclean spirits, crying out loud shrieks, came out of many who were possessed, and many others who were paralyzed or lame were cured. So there was great joy in that city. . . . When they [the people] believed Philip, who was proclaiming the good news about the kingdom of God and the name of Jesus Christ, they were baptized, both men and women. . . .
>
> Now when the apostles at Jerusalem heard that Samaria had accepted the word of God, they sent Peter and John to them. The two went down and prayed for them that they might receive the Holy Spirit (for as yet the Spirit had not come upon any of them; they had only been baptized in the name of the Lord Jesus). Then Peter and John laid their hands on them, and they received the Holy Spirit. (Acts 8:6–7. 12, 14–17)

On their way back to Jerusalem, Peter and John proclaimed the good news to many villages of the Samaritans, but Philip was told by an angel to go south, to the road from Jerusalem to Gaza, where he encountered an Ethiopian eunuch, the queen's treasurer, who was returning from worshiping in Jerusalem. The Ethiopian was riding along in his chariot, reading the prophet Isaiah as he went. The Spirit prompted Philip to join him, and the Ethiopian invited him into his chariot. He asked Philip about a passage in Isaiah:

> Then Philip began to speak, and starting with this scripture, he proclaimed to him the good news about Jesus. As they were going along the road, they came to some water; and the eunuch said, "Look, here is water! What is to prevent me from being baptized?" He commanded the chariot to stop, and both of them, Philip and the eunuch, went down into the water, and Philip baptized him. When they came up out of the water, the Spirit snatched Philip away; the eunuch saw him no more, and went on his way rejoicing. But Philip found himself in Azotus, and as he was passing through the region [up the Mediterranean coast] he proclaimed the good news to all the towns until he came to Caesarea. (Acts 8:35–40)

In this way, manipulated and confirmed by the Holy Spirit, these earliest missionaries spread the good news of Jesus and the kingdom of God up and down Palestine.

On the Road to Damascus

It is at this point that Luke tells the story of Saul's conversion on the road to Damascus. Saul [later called by the Greco-Roman name Paul], a Pharisee and student of the law, who was present at and consented to the stoning of Stephen, violently persecuted the followers of Jesus in Jerusalem and beyond. On his way to Damascus, with a warrant for the arrest of those who were believers in Jesus,

> he fell to the ground and heard a voice saying to him, "Saul, Saul, why do you persecute me." He said, "Who are you, Lord?" The reply came, "I am Jesus, whom you are persecuting. But get up and enter the city, and you will be told what you are to do." (Acts 9:4–6)

A disciple in Damascus, named Ananias, was instructed by the Lord to go to Saul:

The Lord said to him, "Go, for he is an instrument whom I have chosen to bring my name before Gentiles and kings and the people of Israel; I myself will show him how much he must suffer for the sake of my name." So Ananias went and entered the house. He laid his hands on Saul and said, "Brother Saul, the Lord Jesus, who appeared to you on your way here, has sent me so that you may regain your sight and be filled with the Holy Spirit." And immediately . . . his sight was restored. Then he got up and was baptized. (Acts 9:15–18)

Luke has Paul recount this conversion experience two more times in Acts, once to the people gathered at the temple in Jerusalem (22:1–21) and again before King Agrippa in Caesaria (26:1–23).

Peter as Missionary

Luke sets the scene for the mission to the Gentiles by describing Peter, the leader of the apostles, making a pastoral visit to some of the towns that had already been evangelized. He healed a paralytic in the town of Lydda and then restored a dead woman to life in the port city of Joppa. While staying there in the house of Simon, the tanner, Peter was summoned by Cornelius, a Roman centurion, who was a devout and God-fearing man respected by all, to come to his home in Caesarea, just up the coast.

Before Cornelius's emissaries arrived, Peter had a vision of all manner of unclean animals, forbidden to Jews, accompanied by a voice telling Peter to eat them.

But Peter said, "By no means, Lord; for I have never eaten anything that is profane or unclean." The voice said to him again, a second time, "What God has made clean, you must not call profane." This happened three times. (Acts 10:14–16).

Then the Spirit told Peter of the arrival of the three men sent by Cornelius and that he should not hesitate to accompany them (Acts 10:19–20).

Peter and six of the believers from Joppa went up to Cornelius's house in Caesarea, and found a crowd of Cornelius's relatives and

friends. Peter, said to them, "You yourselves know that it is unlaw-
ful for a Jew to associate with or to visit a Gentile, but God has
shown me that I should not call anyone profane or unclean. So
when I was sent for, I came without objection" (Acts 10:28–29).

Cornelius said to Peter, "All of us are here in the presence of
God to listen to all that the Lord has commanded you to say"
(Acts 10:33).

> Then Peter began to speak to them: "I truly understand
> that God shows no partiality, but in every nation anyone
> who fears him and does what is right is acceptable to him.
> You know the message he sent to the people of Israel,
> preaching peace by Jesus Christ—he is Lord of all. That
> message spread throughout Judea, beginning in Galilee
> after the baptism that John announced: how God anointed
> Jesus of Nazareth with the Holy Spirit and with power;
> how he went about doing good and healing all who were
> oppressed by the devil, for God was with him. We are wit-
> nesses to all that he did both in Judea and in Jerusalem.
> They put him to death by hanging him on a tree; but God
> raised him on the third day and allowed him to appear, not
> to all the people, but to us who were chosen by God as
> witnesses, and who ate and drank with him after he rose
> from the dead. He commanded us to preach to the people
> and to testify that he is the one ordained by God as judge
> of the living and the dead. All the prophets testify about
> him that everyone who believes in him receives forgiveness
> of sins through his name."
>
> While Peter was still speaking, the Holy Spirit fell on all
> who heard the word. The circumcised believers who had
> come with Peter were astounded that the gift of the Holy
> Spirit had been poured out even on the Gentiles, for they
> heard them speaking in tongues and extolling God. Then
> Peter said, "Can anyone withhold the water for baptizing
> these people who have received the Holy Spirit just as we
> have?" So he ordered that they be baptized in the name of
> Jesus Christ. (Acts 10:34–48)

Gentiles had been accepted into the followers of Jesus Christ
by the leader of the apostles, with the constant prompting of the

Holy Spirit. Still, Peter would have to answer for this decisive action to the Jewish members of the Jerusalem community upon his return.

> The circumcised believers criticized him, and asked why he had gone to uncircumcised men and eaten with them. Peter explained everything to them, step by step, including his repeated vision. "When they heard this, they were silenced. And they praised God, saying, 'Then God has given even to the Gentiles the repentance that leads to life.'" (Acts 11:18)

The reception of Gentiles was affirmed with finality by this action of the mother church in Jerusalem. The Jesus movement was evolving.

The Church at Antioch

On the very day that Stephen was stoned to death, a severe persecution of the church in Jerusalem caused many of its members to scatter into the countryside of Judea and Samaria. Some of them went as far as Phoenicia, the island of Cyprus, and the city of Antioch. They preached as they migrated, but only to Jews, not to Greeks.

> But among them were some men from Cyprus and Cyrene who, on coming to Antioch, spoke to the Hellenists also, proclaiming the Lord Jesus. The hand of the Lord was with them, and a great number became believers and turned to the Lord. (Acts 11:20–21)

When news of these Greek converts reached Jerusalem, apparently there was concern over how this newly diverse community was being integrated. Were the Mosaic Law and practices being observed? The church of Jerusalem sent Barnabas to observe the church at Antioch. Barnabas was a Levite from Cyprus, who had protected Saul when he came to Jerusalem after his conversion.

> When he [Barnabas] came [to Antioch] and saw the grace of God, he rejoiced, and the exhorted them all to remain faithful to the Lord with steadfast devotion; for he was a

good man, full of the Holy Spirit and of faith. And a great
many people were brought to the Lord. (Acts 11:23–24)

Barnabas sought out Saul, who had gone back to his hometown
of Tarsus, and brought him to Antioch, where they associated
with the church and taught many people for an entire year.
While there, word came to the church at Antioch by means of a
prophet from Jerusalem, who "predicted by the Spirit that there
would be a severe famine over all the world. . . . The disciples
determined that according to their ability, each would send relief
to the believers living in Judea; this they did sending it to the
elders by Barnabas and Saul" (Acts 11:28–30).

The Holy Spirit was active in the Antioch church, in discern-
ing its members' faith and even in prompting their charitable
contributions. "It was in Antioch that the disciples were first
called 'Christians'" (Acts 11:26).

Barnabas and Saul were among the prophets and teachers in
the church at Antioch. "While they were worshiping the Lord
and fasting, the Holy Spirit said, 'Set apart for me Barnabas and
Saul for the work to which I have called them.' Then after fasting
and praying they laid their hands on them and sent them off. So,
being sent out by the Holy Spirit, they went down to Seleucia;
and from there they sailed to Cyprus" (Acts 13:2–4).

The pattern of the missionary activity of Barnabas and Saul
was to go first to the Jewish synagogues, and, depending on
their acceptance or rejection, then to reach out to Gentile audi-
ences. Their route took them to two cities on Cyprus and five
cities in southeast Asia Minor. Their preaching met with both
success and opposition, from their being heralded as gods after
a miracle healing in Lystra to being expelled and stoned outside
the same city. However, the conclusion of their missionary effort
was judged a success. Many had responded to their preaching,
both Jews and Gentiles, and had become believers.

> From there [Attalia] they sailed back to Antioch, where
> they had been commended to the grace of God for the
> work that they had completed. When they arrived, they
> called the church together and related all that God had
> done with them, and how he had opened a door of faith
> for the Gentiles. (Acts 14:26–27)

While the conversion of the Roman centurion Cornelius by Peter might have been considered by some in the Jewish portion of the church to have been an exception, now the door was wide open for Gentile converts from many backgrounds.

The whole of this first missionary journey, beginning and ending in Antioch, was under the aegis of the Holy Spirit, who called Barnabas and Saul forth, sent them out, and accompanied their preaching. Saul, also known by the Greco-Roman name of Paul, was "filled with the Holy Spirit" (Acts 13:9) like Peter and Stephen before him and became an exemplary "Spirit-bearer."

The Council of Jerusalem

After the missionary ventures of Paul and Barnabas and the conversion of the Roman centurion Cornelius and his entourage by Peter, it was clear that the nascent Christian church welcomed Gentile members in addition to its majority of Jewish members. What was not yet clear was under what conditions they were admitted. Were Gentile converts required to submit to circumcision and the dietary and other regulations of Mosaic Law, which many of the Jewish Christians continued to observe? It was a question that went to the heart of the Jewish-Christian relationship.

> Then certain individuals came down [to Antioch] from Judea and were teaching the brothers, "Unless you are circumcised according to the custom of Moses, you cannot be saved." And after Paul and Barnabas had no small dissensions and debate with them, Paul and Barnabas and some of the others were appointed to go up to Jerusalem to discuss this question with the apostles and elders. . . . When they came to Jerusalem, they were welcomed by the church and by the apostles and the elders, and they reported all that God had done with them. But some believers who belong to the sect of the Pharisees stood up and said, "It is necessary for them to be circumcised and ordered to keep the law of Moses."
>
> The apostles and elders met together to consider this matter. After there had been much debate, Peter stood up and said to them, "My brothers, you know that in the early

days God made a choice among you, that I should be the one through whom the Gentiles would hear the good news and become believers. And God, who knows the human heart, testified to them by giving them the Holy Spirit, just as he did to us; and in cleansing their hearts by faith, he has made no distinction between them and us. Now, therefore, why are you putting God to the test by placing on the neck of the disciples a yoke that neither our ancestors nor we have been able to bear? On the contrary, we believe that we will be saved through the grace of the Lord Jesus, just as they will." (Acts 15:1–11)

Paul and Barnabas then spoke to the assembly of the signs and wonders that God worked among the Gentiles through them. When they had finished, James, the leader of the church in Jerusalem, spoke in support of Peter and the two missionaries and announced his decision regarding the council's action: compose a letter for the church at Antioch that would not impose further restrictions on its Gentile members, with four minor exceptions.

Then the apostles and elders, with the consent of the whole church, decided to choose men from among their members and to send them to Antioch with Paul and Barnabas. They sent Judas called Barsabbas, and Silas, leaders among the brothers, with the following letter: "The brothers, both the apostles and elders, to the believers of Gentile origin in Antioch and Syria and Cilicia, greetings. Since we have heard that certain persons have gone out from us, though with no instructions from us, have said things to disturb you and have unsettled your minds, we have decided unanimously to choose representatives and to send them to you, along with our beloved Barnabas and Paul, who have risked their lives for the sake of our Lord Jesus Christ. We have therefore sent Judas and Silas, who themselves will tell you the same things by word of mouth. For it has seemed good to the Holy Spirit and to us to impose on you no further burden than these essentials: that you abstain from what has been sacrificed to idols and from blood and what has been strangled and from fornication. If you keep yourselves from these, you will do well. Farewell."

So they were sent off and went down to Antioch. When they gathered the congregation together, they delivered the letter. When its members read it, they rejoiced at the exhortation. (Acts 15:22–31)

This is the final and formal decision that Gentile Christians did not have to follow the Mosaic Law. It marked the replacement of law with grace, an evolutionary development. It is important to note that it was the unanimous action of not only the apostles and elders in Jerusalem but of the whole Jerusalem church, and especially that they were conscious of acting in concert with the Holy Spirit. Moreover, they sent their decision not only to Antioch, the church where the issue was raised, but to the whole regions of Syria and Cilicia, where Paul and Barnabas had made Gentile converts.

Notice that the argument made in both the instances of centurion Cornelius and his household and in the Gentiles in Antioch was that when God sends the Holy Spirit on people "just as God did for us," how can baptism be withheld from them? The gift of the Spirit is clear evidence of God's acceptance.

This mode for settling matters of doctrine and discipline within the church—with wide participation, prayer, full discussion, and invocation of the Holy Spirit called a conciliar or synodal process—became the model for future decision making.

Paul's Final Missions and Imprisonment

After the crucial decision on "the Gentile question" taken at the Council of Jerusalem, Paul set forth on another set of missions. These occupy the entire remainder of Luke's book of Acts (chapter 15:36—28:31). In this long, adventurous narrative the Holy Spirit is mentioned a few times, and, with one exception, almost in passing.

When Paul and Timothy traveled through Phrygia and Galatia "having been forbidden by the Holy Spirit to speak the word in Asia," they then "attempted to go into Bithynia, but the Spirit of Jesus would not allow them" (Acts 16:6–7). The Spirit guided them to head away from Asia and toward Europe.

In Ephesus, Paul came upon a small band of about twelve disciples and asked them,

"Did you receive the Holy Spirit when you became believers?" They replied, "No, we have not even heard that there is a Holy Spirit." Then he said, "Into what then were you baptized?" They answered, "Into John's baptism." Paul said, "John baptized with the baptism of repentance, telling the people to believe in the one who was to come after him, that is, in Jesus." On hearing this, they were baptized in the name of the Lord Jesus. When Paul had laid his hands on them, the Holy Spirit came upon them, and they spoke in tongues and prophesied. (Acts 19:2–6)

This experience bore obvious echoes of the Pentecost event earlier in Jerusalem.

At the port city of Miletus Paul gave an emotional farewell address to the elders from the church at nearby Ephesus. Paul spoke of his time with them proclaiming, teaching, and testifying

"to both Jews and Greeks about repentance toward God and faith toward our Lord Jesus. And now, as a captive to the Spirit, I am on my way to Jerusalem, not knowing what will happen to me there, except that the Holy Spirit testifies to me in every city that imprisonment and persecutions are waiting for me." (Acts 20:21–23)

He went on to encourage them to carry out their charge in the church. "Keep watch over yourselves and over all the flock, of which the Holy Spirit has made you overseers, to shepherd the church of God that he obtained with the blood of his own Son" (Acts 20:22, 28). The elders' sacred duties were assigned to them by the Holy Spirit of God.

On his journey to Jerusalem, Paul paused at the port city of Tyre for seven days with the disciples. "Through the Spirit they [the local disciples] told Paul not to go Jerusalem" (Acts 21:4). After praying with them on the beach and bidding them farewell, Paul then sailed down the coast to Caesarea. He stayed at the house of Philip, the evangelist, one of "the seven." While there for several days,

a prophet named Agabus, came down from Judea. He came to us and took Paul's belt, bound his own feet and

> hands with it, and said, "Thus says the Holy Spirit, 'This
> is the way the Jews in Jerusalem will bind the man who
> owns this belt and will hand him over to the Gentiles.'"
> [The people] urged Paul not to go up to Jerusalem., Then
> Paul answered, " . . . I am ready not only to be bound but
> even to die in Jerusalem for the name of the Lord Jesus."
> (Acts 21:10–13)

The Holy Spirit gave warnings of the conflicts, suffering, and imprisonment that awaited Paul in Jerusalem, but the warnings did not forbid the journey.

The Spirit's predictions came true. A few days after Paul's arrival in Jerusalem, he encountered violent opposition from a faction of Jews who seized him and tried to kill him. The Roman soldiers intervened, arrested Paul, and eventually sent him to Caesarea to be tried before the Roman governor. He was judged to have done nothing deserving of death or imprisonment, but as a Roman citizen he had appealed to the emperor, so they sent him on the long, dangerous journey to Rome (Acts 21:27—28:16).

After many trials and tribulations, Paul finally arrived in Rome, as a prisoner under guard, but he was allowed to live by himself under house arrest. Three days after he arrived he called together the leaders of the Jews, and they expressed interest in hearing his views.

> After they had fixed a day to meet him, they came to his
> lodgings in great numbers. From morning until evening,
> he explained the matter to them, testifying to the kingdom
> of God and trying to convince them about Jesus both
> from the law of Moses and from the prophets. Some were
> convinced by what he said, while others refused to believe.
> So they disagreed with each other; and as they were leav-
> ing, Paul made one final statement: "The Holy Spirit was
> right in saying about your ancestors through the prophet
> Isaiah, 'Go to this people and say, you will indeed listen,
> but never understand, and you will indeed look and never
> perceive.' . . . Let it be known to you then that this salva-
> tion of God has been sent to the Gentiles; they will listen."

He lived there for two whole years at his own expense and welcomed all who came to him, proclaiming the kingdom of God and teaching about the Lord Jesus Christ with all boldness and without hindrance. (Acts 28:23–26, 28–31)

The Holy Spirit, speaking through Paul quoting Isaiah, confirmed the central message of the Acts of the Apostles, that the gospel message of Jesus triumphed, despite strong opposition. Tradition has it that Paul was killed in Rome during the persecution under the Emperor Nero about the year 67.

The Church at Thessalonica

In his opening address to the Thessalonians, Paul reminded them how God chose them

because our message of the gospel came to you not in word only, but also in power and in the Holy Spirit and with full conviction; just as you know what kind of people we proved to be among you for your sake. And you became imitators of us and of the Lord, for in spite of persecution you received the word with joy inspired by the Holy Spirit, so that you became an example to all the believers in Macedonia and Achaia. (1 Thess 1:5–6)

Paul said that the Thessalonians not only received the Holy Spirit, but that the Spirit was the reason for the depth of their faith conviction as well as the source of their joy, one of the Spirit's gifts.

Later in the letter Paul spoke of the Spirit as an ongoing gift of God, a present and active reality in their lives (1 Thess 4:8). Toward the end of this brief letter Paul urges his readers, "Do not quench the Spirit. Do not despise the words of prophets, but test everything; hold fast to what is good; abstain from every form of evil" (1 Thess 5:19–22). The Holy Spirit's activity in the community apparently took the form of charismatic utterances that sometimes required careful discernment.

In the second letter addressed to the Thessalonians the author made reference to the Holy Spirit as the cause of their sanctification. "We must always give thanks to God for you, brothers and sisters beloved by the Lord, because God chose you as the first fruits for salvation through sanctification by the Spirit and through belief in the truth" (2 Thess 2:13).

The Churches of Galatia

Paul's letter to the communities in the region of Galatia is one of his earliest and angriest letters. The central issue of the letter, and the reason for Paul's anger, is the attempt on the part of some to introduce obedience to the Mosaic Law, especially circumcision, to the churches' commitment to Christ that Paul had preached to them. This passage captures Paul's anger as well as his contrast between the Spirit and the flesh.

> You foolish Galatians! Who has bewitched you? It was before your eyes that Jesus Christ was publicly exhibited as crucified! The only thing I want to learn from you is this: Did you receive the Spirit by doing the works of the law or by believing what you heard? Are you so foolish? Having started with the Spirit are you now ending with the flesh? . . . Well then, does God supply you with the Spirit and work miracles among you by doing the works of the law or by your believing what you heard? . . . Christ redeemed us from the curse of the law by becoming a curse for us—for it is written, "Cursed is everyone who hangs on a tree"—in order that in Christ Jesus the blessing of Abraham might come to the Gentiles, so that we might receive the promise of the Spirit through faith. (Gal 3:1–5, 13–14)

With these scolding words Paul insisted that the promised Spirit is supplied by faith in Jesus Christ, not by doing the works of the Law.

Paul spoke of Christians as children of God. Paul compared the Galatians' previous condition as being under the Mosaic Law, which he likened to a custodian (a slave in a Greek family who led the children to their teachers), who looked after and minded them before the coming of Christ. Having been justified by faith in Jesus Christ, we are adopted children within God's family.

> Therefore the law was our disciplinarian until Christ came,
> so that we might be justified by faith. But now that faith
> has come, we are no longer subject to a disciplinarian, for
> in Christ Jesus you are all children of God through faith.
> . . . When the fullness of time had come, God sent his Son,
> born of a woman, born under the law, in order to redeem
> those who were under the law, so that we might receive
> adoption as children. And because you are children, God
> has sent the Spirit of his Son into our hearts, crying "Abba!
> Father!" So you are no longer a slave but a child, and if a
> child then also an heir, through God. (Gal 3:24–26; 4:4–7)

The Holy Spirit has been given to us and dwells within us, a
participation in divinity. The Spirit enables us to speak to the
Father as children speak to their father.

Further on Paul expanded on the contrast between Spirit and
flesh in the way Christians should live.

> Live by the Spirit, I say, and do not gratify the desires of the
> flesh. For what the flesh desires is opposed to the Spirit, and
> what the Spirit desires is opposed to the flesh; for these are
> opposed to each other, to prevent you from doing what you
> want. But if you are led by the Spirit, you are not subject
> to the law. Now the works of the flesh are obvious: for-
> nication, impurity, licentiousness, idolatry. . . . By contrast
> the fruit of the Spirit is love, joy, peace, patience, kindness,
> generosity, faithfulness, gentleness, and self-control. There
> is no law against such things. And those who belong to
> Christ Jesus have crucified the flesh with its passions and
> desires. If we live by the Spirit, let us also be guided by the
> Spirit. (Gal 5:16–19, 22–25)

Paul urged the Galatians to follow these positive promptings of
the Spirit in the way they behave in their daily lives.

The Church at Corinth

Paul founded the church in the port city of Corinth in about the
year 51, and he wrote this long, complex letter to them with the

loving concern of a father for his children. He described his way of preaching the mysteries of God.

> When I came to you, brothers and sisters, I did not come proclaiming the mystery of God to you in lofty words of wisdom. . . . My speech and my proclamation were not with plausible words of wisdom, but with a demonstration of Spirit and power, so that your faith might rest not on human wisdom but on the power of God. . . .
>
> "What no eye has seen, nor ear heard, nor the human heart conceived, what God has prepared for those who love him"—these things God has revealed to us through the Spirit; for the Spirit searches everything, even the depths of God. . . . No one comprehends what is truly God's except the Spirit of God. Now we have received not the spirit of the world, but the Spirit that is from God, so that we may understand the gifts bestowed on us by God. And we speak of these things in words not taught us by human wisdom but taught by the Spirit, interpreting spiritual things to those who are spiritual.
>
> Those who are unspiritual do not receive the gifts of God's Spirit, for they are foolishness to them, and they are unable to understand them because they are discerned spiritually. (1 Cor 2:1, 4–5, 9–14)

The Holy Spirit, not human wisdom, was the source of Paul's knowledge of the mysteries of God, and it was the Spirit who helped the Corinthians comprehend the gifts God had given them. They had become attuned to the Spirit.

Paul wrote about the church as a spiritual edifice which he helped to build, but then he reminded the Corinthians where they fit in: "Do you not know that you are God's temple and that God's Spirit dwells in you? . . . God's temple is holy, and you are that temple" (1 Cor 3:16–17). In another place Paul used this same image of a temple of the Holy Spirit in reference to the human body:

> Do you not know that your bodies are members of Christ? . . . Or do you not know that your body is a temple of the Holy Spirit within you, which you have from God, and that

you are not your own? For you were bought with a price; therefore glorify God in your body. (1 Cor 6:15, 19–20)

Paul taught the Corinthians that the Holy Spirit dwelled within them, and that they had been cleansed of their previous sins by the Spirit as well as by Jesus Christ:

Do you not know that wrongdoers will not inherit the kingdom of God? . . . And this is what some of you used to be. But you were washed, you were sanctified, you were justified in the name of the Lord Jesus Christ and in the Spirit of our God. (1 Cor 6:9, 11)

Paul introduced his discussion of spiritual gifts within the community by affirming that it is only through the power of the Holy Spirit that the Corinthians can make their baptismal commitment to Christ: "No one can say 'Jesus is Lord' except by the Holy Spirit" (1 Cor 12:3). He then named three general categories of God-given charisms within the community: (1) gifts, (2) services or ministries, and (3) activities or workings, each with its own distinctive divine source. He followed these by enumerating an entire list of different gifts given to individuals by the Holy Spirit for the benefit of the local congregation.

Now there are varieties of gifts, but the same Spirit; and there are varieties of services, but the same Lord, and there are varieties of activities, but the same God who activates all of them in everyone. To each is given the manifestation of the Spirit for the common good. To one is given through the Spirit the utterance of wisdom, and to another the utterance of knowledge according to the same Spirit, to another faith by the same Spirit, to another gifts of healing by the one Spirit, to another the working of miracles, to another prophecy, to another the discernment of spirits, to another various kinds of tongues, to another the interpretation of tongues. All these are activated by one and the same Spirit, who allots to each one individually just as the Spirit chooses.

For just as the body is one and has many members, and all the members of the body, though many, are one body, so it is with Christ. For in the one Spirit we were all baptized into one body—Jews or Greeks, slaves or free—and we were all made to drink of the one Spirit. (1 Cor 12:4–13)

All of these individual abilities, talents, and insights come from the Holy Spirit and are meant to contribute to the good of the whole community, "so that the church may be built up" (1 Cor 14:5). The spirit's gifts are both personal and communal.

Paul went on at length to show how these various gifts must be coordinated and balanced when the community gathers, "for God is a God not of disorder but of peace" (1 Cor 14:5, 33). Clearly there was an awareness of the Spirit's active involvement in the life of the church at Corinth, in virtue of the charismatic gifts given to individual members.

Paul wrote a second, intensely personal letter to the church at Corinth a few years after the first. As an illustration of his sincerity and constancy, Paul called upon God, Christ, and the Spirit. "But it is God who establishes us with you in Christ, and has anointed us, by putting his seal on us and giving us his Spirit in our hearts as a first installment" (2 Cor 1:21–22). God has marked us out for Christ in our baptism, and at the same time God gave us the Holy Spirit to dwell within us as a down-payment on the fullness of our salvation. Later on in this letter, when speaking of our earthly home in anticipation of our future home in heaven, Paul used a similar expression for the role of the Holy Spirit: "He who has prepared us for this very thing is God, who has given us the Spirit as a guarantee" (2 Cor 5:5).

Paul brought up the subject of letters of recommendation, and said that they are not necessary in his case with the Corinthians because "you yourselves are our letter, written on our hearts, to be known and read by all; and you show that you are a letter of Christ, prepared by us, written not with ink, but with the Spirit of the living God, not on tablets of stone, but on tablets of human hearts" (2 Cor 3:2–3). The Spirit had come to them and dwells within them, by means of Paul's teaching and their baptism.

Such is the confidence we have through Christ towards God. Not that we are competent of ourselves to claim anything as coming from us; our competence is from God, who has made us to be ministers of a new covenant, not of letter but of spirit; for the letter kills, but the Spirit gives life.

Now if the ministry of death, chiselled in letters on stone tablets, came in glory so that the people of Israel could not gaze at Moses' face because of the glory of his face, a glory now set aside, how much more will the ministry of the Spirit come in glory?

Now the Lord is the Spirit, and where the Spirit of the Lord is, there is freedom. And all of us, with unveiled faces, seeing the glory of the Lord as though reflected in a mirror, are being transformed into the same image from one degree of glory to another; for this comes from the Lord, the Spirit. (2 Cor 3:4–8, 17–18)

Paul defended his ministry of the new covenant in Christ by contrasting it with the old covenant brought by Moses. The Lord, the Holy Spirit is the Spirit of Christ who has been given to us and works within us.

Paul concluded this stormy and defensive letter to the Corinthians with a trinitarian blessing for them: "The grace of the Lord Jesus Christ, the love of God, and the communion of the Holy Spirit be with all of you" (2 Cor 13:13).

The Church at Rome

Paul's longest and best organized explanation of his thought is a letter to the community of Christians, both Jews and Gentiles, in Rome about the year 57. In a section on which he spoke of our salvation through faith in Jesus Christ, he said that the Holy Spirit in our hearts is both source and proof of God's love for us.

Therefore, since we are justified by faith, we have peace with God through our Lord Jesus Christ, through whom we have obtained access to this grace in which we stand; and we boast in our hope of sharing the glory of God. . . . Hope does not disappoint us, because God's love has been poured into our hearts through the Holy Spirit that has been given to us. (Rom 5:1–2, 5)

Our saving hope, based on our faith in Jesus Christ, is confirmed by God's love for us which we receive and are aware of through the Holy Spirit.

In another place Paul contrasts life according to the Spirit (for those who are in Jesus Christ) and life according to the flesh.

> For the law of the Spirit of life in Christ Jesus has set you free from the law of sin and death. . . . For those who live according to the flesh set their minds on the things of the flesh, but those who live according to the Spirit set their minds on the things of the Spirit. To set the mind on the flesh is death, but to set the mind on the Spirit is life and peace. For this reason the mind that is set on the flesh is hostile to God; it does not submit to God's law—indeed it cannot, and those who are in the flesh cannot please God.
>
> But you are not in the flesh; on the contrary, you are in the Spirit, since the Spirit of God dwells in you. Anyone who does not have the Spirit of Christ does not belong to him. But if Christ is in you, though the body is dead because of sin, the Spirit is life because of righteousness. If the Spirit of him who raised Jesus from the dead dwells in you, he who raised Christ from the dead will give life to your mortal bodies also through his Spirit that dwells in you.
>
> So then, brothers and sisters, we are debtors not to the flesh, to live according to the flesh—for if you live according to the flesh you will die; but if by the Spirit you put to death the deeds of the body, you will live. (Rom 8:2, 5–13)

The indwelling Holy Spirit is not only the source of grace and strength in our struggles with temptation and sin in this life, but also the source of our resurrected life with Christ after death. The Spirit is a vivifying force within us.

Paul abruptly changed his imagery from the spirit-flesh contrast to one of relationship: Christians are children of God by adoption, through the work of the Spirit.

> For all who are led by the Spirit of God are children of God. For you did not receive a spirit of slavery to fall back into fear, but you have received a spirit of adoption. When

we cry "Abba! Father!" it is that very Spirit bearing witness with our spirit that we are children of God, and if children, then heirs, heirs of God and joint heirs with Christ—if, in fact, we suffer with him so that we may also be glorified with him. (Rom 8:14–17)

The gift of the Holy Spirit makes Christians into members of God's family, daughters and sons by adoption, not slaves, but full members of the family and co-heirs with Christ, God's Son.

The revelation of the reality of God's children remains to be seen. Along with all the rest of creation it awaits deliverance from the curse cast by the Lord on Adam because of his disobedience (Gen 3:17–19).

For the creation waits with eager longing for the revealing of the children of God; for the creation was subjected to futility, not by its own will but by the will of the one who subjected it, in hope that the creation itself will be set free from its bondage to decay and will obtain the freedom of the glory of the children of God. We know that the whole creation has been groaning in labor pains until now; and not only the creation, but we ourselves, who have the first fruits of the Spirit, groan inwardly while we wait for adoption, the redemption of our bodies. For in hope we were saved. (Rom 8:19–24)

The Spirit is the pledge, the promise of redemption—not only for individual believers in Jesus Christ, adopted children in God's family, but for all of creation, for the whole created universe. Full redemption, "the freedom of the glory of the children of God" (Rom 8:21) lies ahead, as well as the future of the evolving world in which the children will live. What will it look like? The Spirit summons us toward an evolutionary future.

In the same context Paul pointed out another way in which the Holy Spirit comes to our aid, in our prayers.

Likewise the Spirit helps us in our weakness; for we do not know how to pray as we ought, but that very Spirit intercedes with sighs too deep for words. And God, who searches the heart, knows what is the mind of the Spirit, because the Spirit intercedes for the saints according to the will of God. (Rom 8:26–27)

God recognizes our Spirit-enabled prayer, and it is part of God's overall plan of salvation that the Spirit should play this intrinsic and personal role, teaching us how to communicate with God.

Paul also instructed the Romans that "joy in the Holy Spirit" (Rom 14:17) is one of the conditions of Christian conduct, one that proceeds from the prompting of the indwelling Spirit. Paul spoke of this in the context of the delicate issue of dietary practices (not eating food that is unclean) and the need to have consideration for the consciences of others.

> Let us therefore no longer pass judgment on one another, but resolve instead never to put a stumbling-block or hindrance in the way of another. I know and am persuaded in the Lord Jesus that nothing is unclean in itself; but it is unclean for anyone who thinks it unclean. If your brother or sister is being injured by what you eat, you are no longer walking in love. Do not let what you eat cause the ruin of one for whom Christ died. . . . For the kingdom of God is not food and drink but righteousness and peace and joy in the Holy Spirit. The one who thus serves Christ is acceptable to God and has human approval. (Rom 14:13–15, 17–18)

In the concluding sections of his long letter to the Romans, Paul spoke of the Holy Spirit several times, first as the source of their hope. "May the God of hope fill you will all joy and peace in believing, so that you may abound in hope by the power of the Holy Spirit" (Rom 15:13). Next, he attributed to the Holy Spirit the conversion and sanctification of the Gentiles:

> On some points I have written to you rather boldly by way of reminder, because of the grace given to me by God to be a minister of Christ Jesus to the Gentiles in the priestly service of the gospel of God, so that the offering of the Gentiles may be acceptable, sanctified by the Holy Spirit. In Christ Jesus then, I have reason to boast of my work for God. For I will not venture to speak of anything

except what Christ has accomplished through me to win obedience from the Gentiles, by word and deed, by the power of signs and wonders, by the power of the Spirit of God, so that from Jerusalem and from as far around as Illyricum I have fully proclaimed the good news of Christ. (Rom 15:15–19)

It was the power of the Spirit of God that made Paul's work among the Gentiles effective, from Jerusalem all the way to the west coast of Greece on the Adriatic, and that Paul hoped to extend as far as Spain, with a visit to Rome on the way (Rom 15:22–24). Paul made his final reference to the Holy Spirit in his request for prayers: "I appeal to you brothers and sisters, by our Lord Jesus Christ and by the love of the Spirit, to join me in earnest prayers to God on my behalf. . . . The God of peace be with all of you. Amen" (Rom 15:30, 33).

The Church at Philippi

Phillippi was a prominent Roman city, named for Philip II of Macedon, the father of Alexander the Great. It was located at the northern end of the Aegean Sea, and it was there that Paul established his first Christian community in Europe, about the year 50. His time there was tumultuous, involving his arrest, public beating, imprisonment, and later release (Acts 16:11–40). Paul wrote this letter to the Philippians a few years later while he was in prison in another place. It has been called a letter of joy for its rejoicing of faith in Christ's work of salvation.

Paul rejoiced at the progress of the proclamation of Christ, and then speculated on his own future trial and the assistance he would receive from the Holy Spirit.

Yes, and I will continue to rejoice, for I know that through your prayers and the help of the Spirit of Jesus Christ this will result in my deliverance. It is my eager expectation and hope that I will not be put to shame in any way, but that by my speaking with all boldness, Christ will be exalted now as always in my body, whether by life or by death. For to me, living is Christ and dying is gain. (Phil 1:18–21)

Paul relied on the prayers of his community at Philippi and on the promise of Jesus that the Holy Spirit would be there to help him in his time of trial (Mark 13:9–11; Luke 12:12).

A little later in the letter Paul urged the Philippians to be united in heart and mind.

> If then there is any encouragement in Christ, any consolation from love, any sharing in the Spirit, any compassion and sympathy, make my joy complete: be of the same mind, having the same love, being in full accord and of one mind. (Phil 2:1–2)

Paul reminded the community that its strong and loving fellowship had its source in their participation *(koinonia)* in the Holy Spirit.

In an abrupt change of tone (perhaps occasioned by some recent news from Philippi), Paul warned passionately against some false teachers—he called them "dogs" and "evil-workers." He asserted that, in contrast to their teachings, we "worship in the Spirit of God and boast in Christ Jesus" (Phil 3:3). Christians rely on the Holy Spirit to create within them a new moral life, a way of living pleasing to God.

The Church at Colossae

This short letter to the Colossians was also written from prison by someone who did not know the Christian community directly, but knew of its achievements and difficulties from communications with others. The letter refers several times to the love that bonds the community together and is due to the influence of the Holy Spirit. After a brief greeting, the letter opens with a prayer of thanksgiving:

> In our prayers for you we always thank God, the Father of our Lord Jesus Christ, for we have heard of your faith in Christ Jesus, and the love that you have for all the saints, because of the hope laid up for you in heaven. You have heard of this hope before, in the word of the truth, the gospel that has come to you. Just as it is bearing fruit and growing in the whole world, so it has been bearing fruit

among yourselves from the day you heard it and truly comprehended the grace of God. This you learned from Epaphras, our beloved fellow-servant. He is a faithful minister of Christ on your behalf, and he has made known to us your love in the Spirit. (Col 1:3–8)

The Holy Spirit is the cause and context of the love that holds together the church at Colossae.

The Church at Ephesus

The letter to the Ephesians may have been written by a disciple of the apostle Paul in the late first century (after Paul had been killed). It was probably intended as a circular letter for the churches in Asia Minor. The author opens the letter (or discourse) with a reminder of God the Father's plan of salvation, fulfilled through Christ, and confirmed by the Holy Spirit.

In him [Christ] you also, when you had heard the word of truth, the gospel of your salvation, and had believed in him, were marked with the seal of the promised Holy Spirit; this is the pledge of our inheritance towards redemption as God's own people, to the praise of his glory. (Eph 1:13–14)

Christians are sealed by the Spirit in their baptism, and the Spirit is the pledge or down payment on complete redemption in Christ.

The author celebrated the reconciliation of Jews and Gentiles in Christ:

For he [Christ] is our peace; in his flesh he has made both groups into one and has broken down the dividing wall, that is, the hostility between us. He has abolished the law with its commandments and ordinances, so that he might create in himself one new humanity in place of the two, thus making peace, and might reconcile both groups to God in one body through the cross, thus putting to death that hostility through it. So he came and proclaimed peace to you who were far off and peace to those who were near; for through him both of us have access through one Spirit to the Father. So then you are no longer strangers and aliens, but you are citizens with the saints and also members of the household of God, built upon the foundation of the apostles and prophets, with Christ Jesus himself as the cornerstone. In him the whole structure is joined together and grows into a holy temple in the Lord; in whom you also are built together in the Spirit into a dwelling-place for God. (Eph 2:14–22)

The author of Ephesians used shifting images to describe the achievements of Christ: first, the peacemaker who created "one new humanity" out of two previously hostile groups and reconciled both to God in one body; then as the cornerstone on which is built the household of God, which grows into a holy temple. The Holy Spirit serves as the Christian's contact with the Father in the peaceful scenario of the reconciled communities of the first image, and as the connecting tissue that holds the living stones of the holy temple together in the second image. In both contexts the Spirit plays a vital and vivifying role.

Writing as Paul in prison, the author of this letter describes the source of his knowledge of the mystery of Christ and its inclusion of the Gentiles.

In former generations this mystery was not made known to humankind, as it now has been revealed to his holy apostles and prophets by the Spirit: that is, the Gentiles have become fellow-heirs, members of the same body, and sharers in the promise of Christ Jesus through the gospel. (Eph 3:5–6)

The Holy Spirit is named as the revealer of God's plan to the apostles and prophets who were to proclaim it to all nations.

In a prayer for his readers, the author asks for the indwelling Spirit to strengthen them:

"I bow my knees before the Father. . . . I pray that according to the riches of his glory, he may grant that you may be strengthened in your inner being with power through his Spirit, and that Christ may dwell in your hearts through faith, as you are being rooted and grounded in love.

> Now to him who by the power at work within us is able
> to accomplish abundantly far more than all we can ask or
> imagine, to him be glory in the church and in Christ Jesus
> to all generations, for ever and ever. Amen. (Eph 3:14,
> 16–17, 20–21)

The Holy Spirit is identified as a power source within us, in
our hearts, to enable us to do more than we can even imagine
possible.

The author, again reminding his readers that he writes from
prison, makes this powerful exhortation to unity in the church,
exhibited in both attitudes and beliefs:

> I therefore, the prisoner in the Lord, beg you to lead a life
> worthy of the calling to which you have been called, with
> all humility and gentleness, with patience, bearing with
> one another in love, making every effort to maintain the
> unity of the Spirit in the bond of peace. There is one body
> and one Spirit, just as you were called to the one hope of
> your calling, one Lord, one faith, one baptism, one God
> and Father of all, who is above all, and through all, and
> in all. (Eph 4:1–6)

The Holy Spirit is one and is the source and strength of the
church's unity. The exhortation lists the elements of the church's
unity and concludes with a ringing endorsement of the one,
transcendent God.

In the midst of a series of admonitions to proper Christian
living—avoid speaking falsehoods, put away anger, theft, foul
language, bitterness, malice of all kinds—he adds:

> "And do not grieve the Holy Spirit of God, with which
> you were marked with a seal for the day of redemption."
> (Eph 4:30)

Any offense against another member of the community is a
rebuke to the Spirit that was given to each one at baptism as
"a pledge of our inheritance towards redemption as God's own
people" (Eph 1:13–14).

He urges the Ephesians:

> Do not get drunk with wine, for that is debauchery; but be filled with the Spirit, as you sing psalms and hymns and spiritual songs among yourselves, singing and making melody to the Lord in your hearts, giving thanks to God the Father at all times and for everything in the name of our Lord Jesus Christ. (Eph 5:18–20)

A Spirit-filled life should be joyful and exuberant, as should the community's liturgy, but inebriation is quite another matter.

In the final section of this discourse the author uses the imagery of the battlefield to describe the Christian's struggle with the powers of evil.

> Put on the whole armor of God, so that you may be able to stand against the wiles of the devil. . . . Stand therefore, and fasten the belt of truth around your waist, and put on the breastplate of righteousness. . . . With all of these take the shield of faith, with which you will be able to quench all the flaming arrows of the evil one. Take the helmet of salvation, and the sword of the Spirit, which is the word of God.
>
> Pray in the Spirit at all times in every prayer and supplication. (Eph 6:11, 14, 16–18)

The word of God is the powerful weapon of the Holy Spirit in life's battles against temptation and untruth, but prayer in the Spirit is appropriate in every situation.

Churches of the Pastorals

The three short letters addressed to Timothy and Titus, companions of the apostle Paul, are labeled the pastoral letters because they are written to the pastoral leaders of the churches of Ephesus and the Isle of Crete rather than to those church communities. They were probably composed by a disciple of Paul's about the year 100. These letters contain three references to the Holy Spirit.

The author warns Timothy that false teachers will arise in the "end times" and attempt to deceive believers. He attributes these dire predictions to the Holy Spirit.

> Now the Spirit expressly says that in the last times some
> will renounce the faith by paying attention to deceitful
> spirits and teachings of demons, through the hypocrisy of
> liars whose consciences are seared with a hot iron. (1 Tim
> 4:1–2)

The Holy Spirit is held to be the direct source of these revealed
warnings, spoken by Jesus in Matthew 24:23–24 and by Paul
in Acts 20:29–30.

The author of 2 Timothy, writing as Paul in prison, described
his role as preacher, apostle, and teacher of the gospel of Jesus
Christ. He urges Timothy to be true to what he learned from
Paul.

> Hold to the standard of sound teaching that you have
> heard from me, in the faith and love that are in Christ
> Jesus. Guard the good treasure entrusted to you, with the
> help of the Holy Spirit living in us. (2 Tim 1:13–14)

The Holy Spirit dwells within us and safeguards the faith in Jesus
that we have received.

The author reminds Titus that before the coming of Christ
we were all

> foolish, disobedient, led astray, slaves to various passions
> and pleasures, passing our days in malice and envy, de-
> spicable, hating one another. But when the goodness and
> loving kindness of God our Savior appeared, he saved us,
> not because of any works of righteousness that we had
> done, but according to his mercy, through the water of re-
> birth and renewal by the Holy Spirit. This Spirit he poured
> out on us richly through Jesus Christ our Savior, so that,
> having been justified by his grace, we might become heirs
> according to the hope of eternal life. This saying is sure.
> (Titus 3:3–8)

The Holy Spirit, poured out on us at our baptism, caused us to
be reborn into the new humanity of those saved by the grace
of Christ and to become heirs of the hope of eternal life. Paul

adds his personal assurance, as he does in several places in these pastoral letters, that this teaching is trustworthy.

The Church of the Epistle to the Hebrews

The epistle to the Hebrews, probably written by a disciple of Paul's, is focused on the danger to Jewish Christians of those who wanted to draw them back into some sacrificial practices of the Mosaic Law. The author stresses the preeminence of Christ, his ultimate sacrifice, and his ongoing ministry in heaven.

The author's first reference to the Holy Spirit is in the context of an exhortation to his readers to be faithful to what they have learned about salvation in Christ.

> Therefore we must pay greater attention to what we have heard, so that we do not drift away from it. For if the message declared through angels was valid, and every transgression or disobedience received a just penalty, how can we escape if we neglect so great a salvation? It was declared at first through the Lord, and it was attested to by those who heard him, while God added his testimony by signs and wonders and various miracles, and by gifts of the Holy Spirit, distributed according to his will. (Heb 2:1, 3–4)

God has provided confirmation of the salvific achievement of Jesus Christ in two ways: (1) through signs and wonders and miracles, and (2) through the gifts of the Holy Spirit poured out on members of the community, like those mentioned by Paul in 1 Corinthians 12:4–11, such as wisdom, knowledge, faith, healing, prophecy, discernment of spirits, and tongues.

The Spirit is understood to be the inspirer of the scriptures. Here the author of Hebrews attributes to the Holy Spirit the exhortation to fidelity given to the people of Israel in Psalm 95:

> Therefore, as the Holy Spirit says, today, if you hear his voice, do not harden your hearts as in the rebellion, as on the day of testing in the wilderness, where your ancestors put me to the test, though they had seen my works for forty years. (Heb 3:7–11)

Hebrews presents the warning words of the Psalmist, written several centuries before Christ, as communications from the Holy Spirit. The words are still relevant. He used them as an appeal to his readers for steadfastness in faith. Similarly, when comparing the tabernacle worship of the Mosaic covenant to the sacrifice of Jesus, the author attributes to the Holy Spirit the insight that the ancient rite was incomplete in relationship to Christ's (Heb 9:8; Exod 30:10).

The author of Hebrews includes "sharing in the Holy Spirit" as part and parcel of the process of accepting faith in Christ and experiencing baptism (even for those who later fall away):

> For it is impossible to restore again to repentance those who have once been enlightened, and have tasted the heavenly gift, and have shared in the Holy Spirit, and have tasted the goodness of the word of God and the powers of the age to come, and then have fallen away, since on their own they are crucifying again the Son of God and are holding him up to contempt. (Heb 6:4–6)

The author softens the harshness of this judgment in the passage that follows:

> Even though we speak in this way, beloved, we are confident of better things in your case, things that belong to salvation. For God is not unjust; he will not overlook your work, and the love that you showed for his sake in serving the saints, as you still do. (Heb 6:9–10)

The author of Hebrews invokes the Holy Spirit as the revealer of the prophecy of Jeremiah when comparing the daily repetition of the Mosaic ritual with the one-time nature of Christ's sacrifice.

> It is by God's will that we have been sanctified through the offering of the body of Jesus Christ once for all.
>
> And every priest [of the Mosaic observance] stands day after day at his service, offering again and again the same sacrifices that can never take away sins. But when Christ had offered for all time a single sacrifice for sins, "he sat down at the right hand of God," and since then has been

waiting "until his enemies would be made a footstool for his feet." For by a single offering he has perfected for all time those who are sanctified. And the Holy Spirit also testifies to us, for after saying,

> "This is the covenant that I will make with
>   them
>   after those days, says the Lord:
> I will put my laws in their hearts,
>   and I will write them on their minds." (Heb
>   10:10–17)

he also adds,

> "I will remember their sins and their lawless
>   deeds no more." (Jer 31:31–34)

The new covenant foreseen by the prophet Jeremiah and established by Christ, with the law written on the hearts of believers rather than on tablets of stone, is attributed to the Holy Spirit. Christ's unique sacrifice accomplished the forgiveness of sins.

The Churches of Asia Minor

The apostle Peter, or someone using his name and perhaps living in Rome, wrote two letters to those Christians dispersed among the cities of Asia Minor. The writer opens the first letter with an address and a unique trinitarian formula:

> Peter, an apostle of Jesus Christ, To the exiles of the Dispersion in Pontus, Galatia, Cappadocia, Asia, and Bithynia, who have been chosen and destined by God the Father and sanctified by the Spirit to be obedient to Jesus Christ and to be sprinkled with his blood: May grace and peace be yours in abundance. (1 Pet 1:1–2)

The greeting attributes the predestination of Christians to the Father, their saving sacrifice and gospel leadership to Christ, and their sanctification to the Holy Spirit.

Peter continues this theme of salvation in Christ and the Spirit's roles in it a few lines later:

> Concerning this salvation, the prophets who prophesied of the grace that was to be yours made careful search and inquiry, inquiring about the person or time that the Spirit of Christ within them indicated, when it testified in advance to the sufferings destined for Christ and the subsequent glory. It was revealed to them that they were serving not themselves but you, in regard to the things that have now been announced to you through those who brought you the good news by the Holy Spirit sent from heaven—things into which angels long to look! (1 Pet 1:10–12)

The Old Testament prophets were told by the Holy Spirit, who was also the Spirit of Christ, about the sufferings and glorification of Jesus Christ that were to come. Then it was the same Holy Spirit who sent the apostles to spread the good news of Jesus Christ after his death and resurrection.

Toward the end of this letter Peter urges his readers to be prepared for persecution, which was at hand, but not to fear or abandon hope.

> Beloved, do not be surprised at the fiery ordeal that is taking place among you to test you, as though something strange were happening to you. But rejoice in so far as you are sharing Christ's sufferings, so that you may also be glad and shout for joy when his glory is revealed. If you are reviled for the name of Christ, you are blessed, because the spirit of glory, which is the Spirit of God, is resting on you. (1 Pet 4:12–14)

The Christians who were experiencing hardships because of their faith should count it as a blessing to be able to share in the sufferings of Christ Jesus (as the apostles did in Jerusalem, Acts 5:41). It also means that the Holy Spirit is with them, and that they will rejoice when Christ is revealed to them in glory.

In the second letter of Peter, the only reference to the Holy Spirit is in the context of the second coming of Christ *(parousia).*

Peter reminds his readers that he was present at Christ's transfiguration (Matt 17:1–8) and heard God the Father declare "This is my Son, my Beloved, with whom I am well pleased."

> We ourselves heard this voice come from heaven, while we were with him on the holy mountain.
>   So we have the prophetic message more fully confirmed. . . . First of all you must understand this, that no prophecy of scripture is a matter of one's own interpretation, because no prophecy ever came by human will, but men and women moved by the Holy Spirit spoke from God. (2 Pet 1:17–21)

Genuine prophecy, true communication from God, is not human invention, but rather is the inspiration of the Holy Spirit, revealed in a community of individuals, voiced by individuals who grasp it personally.

The Church of the Letter of Jude

A person named Jude, brother of James, who was the early leader of the Jerusalem community, wrote a letter to an unknown Christian community where there were dangers from false teachers. In warning his audience against these evildoers, Jude urges them to be attentive to the Holy Spirit.

> But you, beloved, must remember the predictions of the apostles of our Lord Jesus Christ; for they said to you, "In the last time there will be scoffers, indulging their own ungodly lusts." It is these worldly people, devoid of the Spirit, who are causing divisions. But you, beloved, build yourselves up on your most holy faith; pray in the Holy Spirit; keep yourselves in the love of God; look forward to the mercy of our Lord Jesus Christ that leads to eternal life. (Jude 17–21)

Jude warns that those who do not recognize the Spirit of God cause divisions in the community, and he exhorts his readers to pray in the Holy Spirit.

The Church of the Johannine Epistles

The letters in the New Testament attributed to the apostle John, but composed by someone of his "school," are related to the Gospel of John and probably originate from the same church community. The first of these letters, really more of a treatise than a letter, is an extended exhortation on authentic Christology and its connection to good Christian living. The author assures the members of the community that they already have the truth since they have been anointed with the Holy Spirit.

> You have been anointed by the Holy One [the Spirit], and all of you have knowledge. I write to you, not because you do not know the truth, but because you know it. . . . Let what you heard from the beginning abide in you. If what you heard from the beginning abides in you, then you will abide in the Son and the Father. . . . As for you, the anointing that you received from him abides in you, and so you do not need anyone to teach you. But as his anointing teaches you about all things, and is true and is not a lie, and just as it has taught you, abide in him. (1 John 2:20–21, 24, 27)

See also John 14:26: "The Advocate, the Holy Spirit, whom the Father will send in my name, will teach you everything, and will remind you of all that I have said to you."

A little further on he speaks of the commandment of love in practical terms:

> Little children, let us love, not in word or speech, but in truth and action. . . . Beloved, if our hearts do not condemn us, we have boldness before God; and we receive from him whatever we ask, because we obey his commandments and do what pleases him.
>
> And this is his commandment, that we should believe in the name of his Son Jesus Christ and love one another, just as he has commanded us. All who obey his commandments abide in him, and he abides in them. And by this we know that he abides in us, by the Spirit he has given us. . . .

> By this we know that we abide in him and he in us,
> because he has given us of his Spirit. (1 John 3:18, 21–24;
> 4:13)

Christians who have faith in Jesus Christ and try to show love
for one another are assured that they are truly "in Christ" by the
fact that they have been given the Holy Spirit.

The author of 1 John warns readers that not every manifestation of the spirit is from God and offers them the way to discern
the spirit of truth from the spirit of deceit:

> Beloved, do not believe every spirit, but test the spirits to
> see whether they are from God; for many false prophets
> have gone out into the world. By this you know the Spirit
> of God: every spirit that confesses that Jesus Christ has
> come in the flesh is from God, and every spirit that does
> not confess Jesus is not from God. (1 John 4:1–3)

The Holy Spirit affirms that Jesus Christ achieved our salvation
by taking on our humanity, our flesh and blood.

Near the end of this discourse the author celebrates the fact
that the believing Christian who is "the one who believes that
Jesus is the Son of God" is "the victor over the world."

> This is the one who came by water and blood, Jesus Christ,
> not with the water only, but with the water and the blood.
> And the Spirit is the one that testifies, for the Spirit is the
> truth. There are three that testify, the Spirit and the water
> and the blood, and these three agree. (1 John 5:5–8)

The Holy Spirit, the Truth, is the source of belief in Christ,
from his baptism (water) by John to his crucifixion (blood and
water), and is confirmed by Jesus's own exclamation, "Let the
one who believes in me drink. Out of the believer's heart shall
flow rivers of living water." . . . He said this about the Spirit,
which believers in him were to receive" (John 7:37–39). The
Johannine community was instructed by the Spirit, who had
been given to them, about the meaning of Jesus and his work
of salvation.

The Churches of the Book of Revelation

The book of Revelation is unique within the New Testament. It is a form of prophetic literature that claims to reveal the hidden things of God, especially about events in the future. It employs symbolic imagery, sometimes wildly exaggerated, to convey ideas or happenings in the future. This example of apocalyptic literature was composed toward the end of the first century by a person named John, probably of the Johannine school of the author of John's Gospel and letters, living on the Isle of Patmos, for the purpose of giving encouragement and hope to Christians at a time of persecution, by pointing out Christ's ultimate victory even over death itself.

The first section of Revelation, after a brief prologue, describes the author's vision and the instructions he received from the risen Lord.

> I, John, your brother who share with you in Jesus the persecution and the kingdom and the patient endurance, was on the island called Patmos because of the word of God and the testimony of Jesus. I was in the Spirit on the Lord's day, and I heard behind me a voice like a trumpet saying, "Write in a book what you see and send it to the seven churches, to Ephesus, to Smyrna, to Pergamum, to Thyatira, to Sardis, to Philadelphia, and to Laodicea." (Rev 1:9–11)

These seven churches were all in Asia Minor, not far from Ephesus, in what is today the eastern part of Turkey. The cities were in sequence on a major road, so the individual letters could have formed a circular letter carried from one city to the next. The powerful vision of the risen Christ dictated a short letter to each of the churches, praising its virtues but also pointing out its failings, needed corrections, and an exhortation. Although each letter is different and specific to the named church, probably the number seven, a perfect number, indicates that the message of the later visions was intended for the entire church.

Each of the letters is addressed to "the angel of the church in [the name of the city]." Angels were seen to be presiding spirits over nations or communities. And each of the letters closes with the statement, "Let anyone who has an ear listen to what the Spirit is saying to the churches" (Rev 2:7, 11, 17, 29; 3:6, 13, 22). Thus the words spoken by the risen Jesus Christ are also the words of the Holy Spirit. This implies that the glorified Jesus is equivalent to the Spirit, at least in relation to Christians. ("Now the Lord is the Spirit"—2 Cor 3:17.)

In the midst of a vision of angels coming to announce God's judgment, especially the "torment with fire and sulfur" (Rev 14:10) for "those who worship the beast and his images" (Rev 14:9), there is a counterpoint of good news:

> And I heard a voice from heaven saying, "Write this: Blessed are the dead who from now on die in the Lord," "Yes," says the Spirit, "they will rest from their labors, for their deeds follow them." (Rev 14:13)

It was a common conviction that people's actions followed them after their death as witnesses before the judgment seat of God. Here that idea is voiced by the Spirit of God.

The final section of the book of Revelation is devoted to a vision of the new creation, "a new heaven and a new earth," and in it "the holy city, the new Jerusalem, coming down out of heaven from God, prepared as a bride adorned for her husband" (Rev 21:1–2).

> And I heard a loud voice from the throne saying,
>
> > "See, the home of God is among mortals.
> > He will dwell with them;
> > they will be his peoples,
> > and God himself will be with them. . . .
>
> And the one who was seated on the throne said, "See I am making all things new. . . . To the thirsty I will give water as a gift from the spring of the water of life." (Rev 21:3, 5, 6)

Then an angel took the author to

a great, high mountain and showed me the holy city Jerusalem coming down out of heaven from God. . . . Then the
angel showed me the river of the water of life, bright as
crystal, flowing from the throne of God and of the Lamb
through the middle of the street of the city. On either side
of the river is the tree of life with its twelve kinds of fruit,
producing its fruit each month; and the leaves of the tree
are for the healing of the nations. (Rev 21:10; 22:1–2)

At the very end of the book is an epilogue containing this message:

It is I, Jesus, who sent my angel to you with this testimony
for the churches. . . .

> The Spirit and the bride say, "Come."
> And let everyone who hears say, "Come."
> And let everyone who is thirsty come.
> Let anyone who wishes take the water of life as
>   a gift. (Rev 22:16–17)

This eschatological vision of a new heaven and a new earth is
a symbolic version of the "renewal of all things" predicted by
Jesus "when the Son of Man is seated on his throne of glory"
(Matt 19:28), after the work of salvation is complete. The "new
Jerusalem adorned as bride" is a symbol of the church, the bride
of Christ. The "water of life" or "life-giving water" in the New
Testament is a frequent symbol of the Holy Spirit. Here, in the
final words of John's Revelation, Jesus, the Spirit, and the church
invite all who await the second coming of Christ to partake of
the water of life.

Summary

After the ascension of Jesus Christ his followers formed local
communities, in Jerusalem, Antioch, Samaria, and eventually in
towns and cities around the Mediterranean basin. The New Testament writings outside of the four Gospels reveal much about
these communities and the activities of the Holy Spirit within

them. These varied writings, from the Acts of the Apostles to the book of Revelation, tell us what the authors and their readers believed about the interventions of the Spirit.

At Pentecost the Spirit was given to the disciples with the sound of wind and tongues of fire and made them able to speak in foreign languages. Peter, in explaining this event, told his hearers to repent and be baptized, that their sins would be forgiven, and that they would receive the gift of the Holy Spirit. Peter and the apostles healed many in and around Jerusalem in the name of Jesus and said that the Holy Spirit, "whom God has given to those who obey him" (Acts 5:32), was witness to these miracles.

Stephen, the first martyr, was "filled with the Holy Spirit" at the time he spoke of his vision of Jesus at God's right hand prior to his being stoned to death. Peter and John went to the newly baptized converts in Samaria and laid hands on them, and they received the Holy Spirit (for as yet the Spirit had not come upon them). Saul, on his way to Damascus to persecute the church, fell from his horse and was blinded. He was filled with the Holy Spirit in Damascus as he regained his sight by the laying on of hands by Ananias.

The Holy Spirit fell upon the members of Cornelius's household while Peter spoke to them in Caesarea. The Holy Spirit guided the selection and sending of Barnabas and Saul from Antioch to Cyprus and the cities of Asia Minor. The Council of Jerusalem resolved the Gentile question with the assent of the Holy Spirit. The Spirit guided the apostle Paul and his companions on their missionary journeys.

Thessalonians received the word with joy inspired by the Spirit, and the Spirit sanctified them. Paul spoke to the Galatians about living as children of God, having received the Spirit of God's Son into their hearts, crying "Abba!, Father!" Paul told the Corinthians that they were God's temple, God's Spirit dwelled within them; their various gifts were from the Spirit for the benefit of the community; they were sanctified in the name of the Lord Jesus Christ and in the Spirit of our God; they have been given the Spirit as a first installment (or guarantee) of their salvation.

To the Romans, Paul wrote: "God's love has been poured into our hearts through the Holy Spirit" (5:5); "live according to the

Spirit" (8:5); the Spirit teaches us how to pray and intercedes for us; the Gentiles too have been sanctified by the Holy Spirit: become co-heirs, members of the same body, sharers in the promise of Jesus Christ.

In 2 Timothy we read, "Hold to the standard of sound teaching that you have heard from me" with the help of the Holy Spirit. The letter to the Hebrews attributes to the Holy Spirit the inspiration of the scriptures. The author of 1 Peter refers to the sanctification by the Spirit and states that the Spirit of God rests upon the members of the community. The letters of John remind us that it is by the Spirit Christ has given us that we know that Christ abides in us and we in him. The book of Revelation invites everyone to come and drink of the life-giving water, the Holy Spirit, "from the river of the water of life, bright as crystal, flowing from the throne of God and of the Lamb" (22:1), in the holy city Jerusalem.

Chapter 2

The Evolutionary Force: Post-Biblical Explorations of the Spirit

The Early Church Fathers

After tracing the biblical history of the Holy Spirit through the Old Testament, the revelations of Jesus of Nazareth, and the early Christian communities to which New Testament writings were directed or from which they emanated, we now turn to the post-biblical record. This path follows the leading Christian writers, roughly from the early second century to the mid-fifth century, that is, from the earliest post–New Testament authors to the death of Augustine. That includes two crucial councils: Nicaea (325) and Constantinople (381). Then we trace the *Filioque* controversy (that the Holy Spirit proceeded from the Father *and* from the Son) from its beginning in the sixth century to the two ecumenical councils (Second Lyon, 1274; and Basel/Ferrara/Florence, 1439) that tried mightily to settle it.

This long trail is not easy to follow. It isn't a straight line. The records are scarce and sketchy at times, especially at the beginning of this period. The church was growing and spreading, but it was also subject to severe persecution at the hands of some of the Roman emperors, and it suffered from internal conflicts that we now call heresies or schisms.

The Apostolic Fathers

The earliest of the post-biblical Christian authors are described as *apostolic* because they either claimed or were assumed to have association with one of the original apostles of Jesus. For example, the first of them, Clement of Rome, a bishop, was (at least possibly) a convert of the apostle Peter. He wrote a letter late in the first century to the church at Corinth, which was having a dispute over its local leadership. In this letter Clement affirmed the role of the Holy Spirit in the inspiration of Old Testament scriptures. He also spoke of the Spirit in personal terms and in tandem with the Father and the Son, acknowledging that they are separate and divine (Burgess, 17).

Ignatius, the bishop of Antioch in about 110, was condemned to death under Emperor Trajan and sent to Rome to die. On his way he wrote a series of letters to the churches he encountered, including Ephesus, Philadelphia, and Smyrna. In these letters he spoke of the work of the Spirit in the churches, conferring gifts (charisms) aplenty and serving as a rope that lifts persons from earth to heaven. He linked the gift of prophecy to the offices of bishop, presbyter, and deacon (Burgess, 20).

Polycarp, the bishop of Smryna (one of the towns on the eastern Aegean sea), died a martyr about 155, and as he did so he uttered the first trinitarian doxology (prayer of praise): "I praise you, I bless you, I glorify you through the eternal and heavenly High Priest, Jesus Christ, your beloved Son, through whom be glory to you with Him and with the Holy Spirit both now and through ages yet to come" (Jurgens I, 31).

A guide for catechumens, called the *Didache* or the *Teaching of the Twelve Apostles*, of unknown authorship, was written about 140 and widely circulated thereafter. It didn't speak much about the Holy Spirit, but it clearly presented the baptismal formula, "in the name of the Father, and of the Son, and of the Holy Spirit" (Jurgens I, 2). It also spoke of itinerant teachers, prophets, and apostles (missionaries) in addition to the bishops and deacons elected from among the community members who were to serve the church as prophets and teachers. The traveling ministers were subject to discernment: "If he asks for money he is a false prophet." "Not everyone who speaks in a spirit is a prophet, unless he has the behavior of the Lord. By his behavior, then, the false prophet and the true prophet shall be known" (Jurgens I, 4).

The *Epistle of Barnabas*, a theological tract of unknown authorship (Barnabas was one of Paul's companions on his missionary journeys), was written in the first part of the second century, possibly in Alexandria. In it the author affirms the functions of inspiration and prophecy of the Holy Spirit in the Old Testament as well as the gifts of personal prophecy and indwelling under the New Covenant. The body of the baptized, as in Christ himself, is considered to be the vessel or dwelling place of the Spirit (Burgess, 22).

The Shepherd of Hermas, an apocalyptic tract, was probably written in Rome toward the middle of the second century. Hermas, the author of these visions, was reputedly the brother of Pius, the bishop of Rome. Hermas was carried away by the Holy Spirit when he saw the visions, and he stressed that Christians must prove by their conduct that they have the gifts of the Spirit. The Holy Spirit was seen as the teacher and sanctifier of believers. At one point Hermas quotes the angel of repentance, "I wish to explain to you what the Holy Spirit showed you when he spoke to you in the form of the Church; for that Spirit is the Son of God" (Jurgens I, 36). In at least this passage Hermas seemed not to distinguish between the Son and the Spirit (Burgess, 22–24; Quasten I, 99–100).

Summary

These earliest post–New Testament writers, the apostolic fathers, carried on the revelations of the New Testament for the most part but did not advance far beyond them in their understandings of the Holy Spirit and its operations. However, they clearly affirm the Holy Spirit in their belief and prayers.

The Apologists

The second generation of Christian authors, after the New Testament writers and the apostolic fathers, are referred to as *apologists.* They attempted a defense of this new religion in the face of strong attacks from the defenders of paganism, the official cult, and from those who saw Christianity as a threat to the Roman Empire. They mounted this defense (1) by extolling the virtues of their belief in Christ and the exemplary lives of their Christian communities and (2) by criticizing the philosophies and claims of the pagans. These were the church's first theologians.

Justin Martyr, born in Palestine of pagan parents about the year 100, studied various philosophies before becoming a convert to Christianity. He traveled about as an itinerant teacher and then founded a school in Rome. He was martyred there by beheading about the year 165. Justin was a prolific writer, and perhaps the most prominent of the early apologists, but many of his works have been lost.

Justin linked the three persons, Father, Son, and Holy Spirit, but in trying to coordinate their relationships, he sometimes leaned toward subordinating the second two to the first, at least in rank and function, if not in essence. He spoke of his fellow Christians as recipients of the gift of prophecy and other gifts of the Spirit. Justin also saw the Spirit as active in the process of our regeneration and redemption. He said that the Spirit was the power of God, and the church is holy because God dwells in it in the person of the Holy Spirit (Burgess, 28–29).

Tatian the Syrian was a disciple of Justin's, born a pagan in Syria, and probably converted at Justin's school in Rome; later he returned to Syria and became a Christian Gnostic. Tatian believed that the Holy Spirit was God's representative within the soul, but not in every soul or even every Christian soul, but only within some of the just; the Spirit takes up its abode in the souls of those who live justly and is united with their souls. The Spirit fortifies the soul against evil spirits, and persons are healed by having recourse to the power of God (Burgess, 30; Jurgens I, 64).

Athenagoras of Athens, a contemporary of Tatian, was the most eloquent of the early apologists. Among his works, he wrote *Supplication for the Christians* to the Roman emperors about the year 177. He spoke of the Holy Spirit as an effluence of God, "flowing from him, and returning back again like the beam of the sun," operating in the prophets, "who moved the mouths of the prophets like musical instruments." He wrote of Christians speaking "of God the Father, and of God the Son, and of the Holy Spirit, and declaring both their power in union, and their distinction in order" (Quasten I, 229, 233).

Theophilus of Antioch, the sixth bishop of Antioch, wrote shortly after the year 180. He was the first to use the word *trinity* (*triás* in Greek) for the union of three divine persons in one God. He spoke of them as "God, his Word *(Logos)*, and his Wisdom."

He said that the Spirit was the life-giving power at creation. He held that the evangelists of the New Testament were inspired by the Holy Spirit just as were the prophets of the Old Testament (Quasten I, 236–39; Burgess, 32).

In their efforts to defend their faith, the apologists continued to search for its meaning.

Irenaeus of Lyons

Irenaeus of Lyons, the most important theologian of the second century, was born about 140, probably in Smyrna, where he studied under Polycarp, the bishop. He has been called the founder of Christian theology. He migrated to Lyons in France and in a short time was elected bishop of that city. He was a prolific writer, but many of his writings have been lost. His most celebrated surviving work is *Adversus Haereses* ("Against Heresies"), a lengthy composition in which he attempts to refute the errors and attacks against the faith in his day (180–99), especially the various forms of Gnosticism.

Irenaeus spoke of the Son and the Holy Spirit as the two "hands of God," both cooperating in the economy of salvation, the Holy Spirit inspiring the prophets in service to the Son, all of this ordered by the Father. The Word and the Wisdom were present and operative in creation. Humankind was molded at the beginning by the hands of God, that is, by the Son and the Holy Spirit, after the image and likeness of God.

Irenaeus described the faith of the church in these terms:

> The Church, although scattered over the whole world even to its extremities, received from the apostles and their disciples the faith in one God, the Father Almighty, maker of heaven and earth, . . . and in one Christ Jesus, the Son of God who became incarnate for our salvation, and in the Holy Spirit, who by the prophets proclaimed the dispensation, the advent, the virgin birth, the passion and resurrection from the dead, the bodily ascension of the well-beloved Christ Jesus Our Lord into heaven, and his *parousia* (advent) from the heavens to the glory of the Father. (Quasten I, 300)

Irenaeus held that the believer is redeemed into Christ through the regenerating power of the Holy Spirit and that the Spirit is present and active in the church: "For where the church is, there is the Spirit of God, and where the Spirit of God is, there is the church, and every kind of grace, but the Spirit is truth" (Burgess, 60). The Holy Spirit is the means of confirming our faith, and the ladder of ascent to God. Irenaeus was also convinced that the Spirit was active in the church through the gifts *(charismata)* given to believers—prophecy, tongues, healing, and visions.

He compared the Holy Spirit to the water that is necessary to make wheat into bread and for a tree to bring forth fruit—the Paraclete makes us ready for God. Irenaeus commented on Paul's words to the Corinthians: "Do you not know that you are God's temple, and that God's spirit dwells in you?" (1 Cor 3:16). "He plainly says, then, that the body is a temple in which the Spirit dwells" (Jurgens I, 100).

Irenaeus distinguished the three persons of the Trinity in this way:

> And thus it is shown that there is one God the Father, who is above all and through all and in all. The Father is indeed above all, and He is the Head of Christ. But the Word is through all, and He is the Head of the Church. The Spirit, however, is in us all, and He is the Living Water which the Lord grants to those who rightly believe in Him and love Him and who know that there one Father, who is above all and through all and in us all. (Jurgens I, 101)

It was by refinements such as this that Irenaeus expanded our understanding of the Trinity.

Tertullian

Tertullian was born in Carthage, North Africa, of pagan parents, in about 155. He became an accomplished lawyer, an advocate in Rome. He converted to Christianity in about 193, and from that time until about 220 he devoted himself to writing in defense of and dialogue with Christian beliefs and practices. Around 207 he began to move toward the Montanists, and by 213 he had joined that group. The Montanists, whom mainline Christians considered to be a heretical sect, expected the imminent destruction of the world and sought to live their religious lives in complete abandonment of the world and its pleasures.

In regard to his teachings about the Holy Spirit, Tertullian was convinced that the Spirit was present and active, along with God the Father and God the Son, in the creation of the universe. "And to the Word, the Reason and Power through which . . . God fashioned all things, we do indeed ascribe Spirit as its proper substance, in which Spirit the Word indwells to give utterance, and Reason is present in order to arrange, and Power presides for the purpose of bringing to completion" (Jurgens I, 114).

It is a "rule of faith" that the Creator brought forth all things out of nothing through his Word, and brought down from the Spirit and power of God the Father into the virgin Mary, and was made flesh in her womb, and came forth as Jesus Christ. "He preached a new law and a new promise of the kingdom of heaven; worked miracles; was crucified, rose again on the third day; and having ascended into heaven, sat at the right of the Father; sent the Holy Spirit with vicarious power to lead those who believe" (Jurgens I, 120).

"The apostles," Tertullian wrote, "obtained the promised power of the Holy Spirit for miracles and eloquence, and after first bearing witness to faith in Jesus Christ in Judea, and having established Churches there, they next went forth into the world and preached the same doctrine of the same faith to the gentiles" (Jurgens I, 120).

Speaking of the water of baptism, Tertullian wrote:

The Spirit who in the beginning hovered over the waters would continue to linger as an influence upon the waters. . . . All waters, therefore . . . are suitable, after God has been invoked, for the sacrament of sanctification. The Spirit immediately comes from heaven upon the waters, and rests upon them, making them holy of Himself; and having been thus sanctified they absorb at the same time the power of sanctifying . . . since we are defiled by sins, as if by dirt, we are washed in water. (Jurgens I, 126)

Tertullian added that the form for baptism was prescribed, "Go, teach the nations, washing them in the name of the Father and of the Son and of the Holy Spirit" (Jurgens I, 126).

Somewhat later, as Tertullian began to lean toward Montanism he spoke again of the "rule of faith" that is "one, alone unchangeable, and irreformable." He then quotes the creed and adds: "This law of faith remaining the same, the other points of discipline or practice admit newer correction, since, of course, the grace of God works and perfects up to the end." Then he went on to ask, "What, then, is the administrative office of the Paraclete, if not this?—that discipline be directed, that the Scriptures be revealed, that the understanding be reshaped, and that progress be made to those things which are better" (Jurgens I, 137). He seemed to say that the Holy Spirit should lead the ongoing reform of the church.

When solidly in the Montanist camp, Tertullian still used language about the Trinity that resounded later in the Council of Nicaea:

> We do indeed believe that there is only one God; but we believe that under this dispensation, or as we say, *oikonomia* (economy), there is also a Son of this one only God, His Word, who proceeded from Him, and through whom all things were made. . . . We believe that he sent down from the Father, in accord with His own promise, the Holy Spirit, the Paraclete, the Sanctifier of the faith of those who believe and in the Son and in the Holy Spirit.
>
> The mystery of the *oikonomia* is safeguarded, for the Unity is distributed in a Trinity. Placed in order the Three are Father, Son, and Spirit. They are Three, however, not in condition, but in degree; not in substance, but in form; not in power, but in kind; of one substance, however, and one condition, and one power, because He is one God, of whom these degrees and forms and kinds are taken into account in the name of the Father, and of the Son, and of the Holy Spirit.
>
> I believe that the Spirit proceeds not otherwise than from the Father through the Son. (Jurgens I, 154)

Tertullian went on to explain that the Father and Son and Spirit are inseparable, but the Father is other, and the Son is other, and the Spirit is other. They are other not by diversity but by distribution, not by division but by distinction. They are one in substance, here called *Trinitas* for the first time in Latin (Jurgens I, 155).

Tertullian was also the first to use the Latin word *persona* of the Holy Spirit.

Clement of Alexandria

Clement was born about 150, probably in Athens, to pagan parents. He converted to Christianity and traveled widely in search of deeper knowledge of his faith. He found the wise teacher he sought in the school for catechumens in the intellectually dynamic city of Alexandria, settled there, and eventually became the head of the school himself in about 200. Shortly thereafter he was forced to flee from imperial persecution, and he died in Cappadocia about 215. He was very well educated and a prolific writer who used Greek philosophy in service to the Christian faith.

Clement focused his theological system on the Logos, the creator of the universe and the manifestation of God. He was convinced that there is only one universal church, just as there is one God the Father, one divine Word, and one Holy Spirit (Quasten II, 20, 24).

When speaking of the flesh and blood of Christ in the Eucharist, Clement wrote:

> The flesh figuratively represents to us the Holy Spirit; for the flesh [of Jesus] was created by Him. The blood points out to us the Word, for as rich blood the Word has been infused into life; and the union of both is the Lord, . . . the Lord who is Spirit and Word.
>
> To drink the blood of Jesus, is to become partaker of the Lord's immortality; the Spirit being the energetic principle of the Word, as the blood is of the flesh.
>
> Accordingly, as wine is blended with water, so is the Spirit with man. And the one, the mixture of wine and

water, nourishes to faith; while the other, the Spirit, conducts to immortality.

And the mixture of both—of the drink and of the Word—is called the Eucharist, renowned and glorious grace; and they who by faith partake of it are sanctified both in body and soul. (Quasten II, 30–31)

By the will of the Father, the divine mixture, man, is mystically united to the Spirit and to the Word. (Jurgens I, 179)

Clement held that believers are inspired by the Spirit:

But we assert that the Holy Spirit inspires him who has believed. The Platonists hold that the mind is an effluence of divine dispensation in the soul, and they place the soul in the body. For it is expressly said by Joel, one of the twelve prophets, "And it shall come to pass after these things, I will pour out of My Spirit on all flesh, and your sons and daughters shall prophesy." But it is not as a portion of God that the Spirit is in each of us. But how this dispensation takes place, and what the Holy Spirit is, shall be shown by us in the books on prophecy, and in those on the soul. (Burgess, 71–72)

Clement wrote of the establishment of churches in the region of Ephesus by the apostle John, under the direction of the Holy Spirit: "Upon being invited, he went even to the neighboring cities of the pagans, here to appoint bishops, there to set in order whole Churches, and there to ordain to the clerical estate such as were designated by the Spirit" (Jurgens I, 187).

Origen

Born the eldest child in a large Christian family in the environs of Alexandria in about 185, Origen went on to become the outstanding scholar of the early church. He was the head of the school for catechumens in Alexandria and later the head of a similar school in Caesarea. He was arrested, imprisoned and tortured in the persecution of Emperor Decius in 250, and died in Tyre in 253. He was an amazingly prolific writer, thanks in part to a team of stenographers and copyists who took his dictation. The number of his works—including biblical criticism, exegetical books, homilies, commentaries, apologetical works, dogmatic writings, spirituality, and letters—range into the thousands. Origen was immensely influential, but his errors—preexistence of human souls, overreliance on allegorical interpretation of the scriptures—and his enemies succeeded in having him excommunicated (by local synods in 230 and 231). Fifteen of his teachings were condemned long after his death at a general council in Constantinople (553).

On the status of the Holy Spirit within the Trinity, Origen was not entirely consistent, saying in one place that "the Holy Spirit is the most excellent and the first in order of all that was made by the Father through Christ," and in another, "that there is no difference in the Trinity, but that which is called the gift of the Spirit is made known through the Son, and operated by God the Father." In still another place Origen stated "up to the present time we have been able to find no statement in holy Scripture in which the Holy Spirit could be said to be made or created" (Burgess, 73–74).

At times, for Origen, the Son and the Holy Spirit are intermediaries between the Father and creatures. "We say that the Savior and the Holy Spirit are without comparison and are very much superior to all things that are made, but also that the Father is more above them than they are themselves above creatures even the highest." For these and similar remarks, Origen was accused of subordinationism. He proposed a hierarchical order in the Trinity and regarded the Holy Spirit as ranking below the Son (Quasten II, 79).

In speaking of the apostolic preaching, Origen wrote:

They handed it down that the Holy Spirit is associated in honor and dignity with the Father and the Son. In His case, however, it is not clearly distinguished whether or not He was born, or even whether or not He is or is not to be regarded as a Son of God. . . . It is most clearly taught in the Churches that this Spirit inspired each one of the holy men, whether Prophets or Apostles; and that there was not one Spirit in the men of old, and another in those who were inspired after the coming of Christ. (Jurgens I, 191)

It is of ecclesiastical teaching that the Scriptures were written through the Spirit of God, . . . the opinion of the whole Church is one: that the whole Law is indeed spiritual, the spiritual meaning which the Law conveys, however, is not known to all, but only to those on whom the grace of the Holy Spirit is bestowed in the word of wisdom and knowledge. . . . The Holy Spirit is a Sanctifying Power, in which all are said to participate who have deserved to be sanctified by His grace. (Jurgens I, 192)

Origen wrote that the Father, the Son, and the Holy Spirit are said to transcend all time, all ages, all eternity, and, that the three cooperate in the work of human salvation:

He who is regenerated by God unto salvation has to do both with Father and Son and Holy Spirit, and does not obtain salvation unless with the cooperation of the entire Trinity. . . . It is impossible to become partaker of the Father or the Son without the Holy Spirit. (Burgess, 75)

In writing about baptism, Origen said, "Formerly [in the Old Testament] there was Baptism, in an obscure way in the cloud and in the sea; now, however, in full view, there is regeneration in water and in the Holy Spirit" (Jurgens I, 206).

Yet Origen held that the Holy Spirit also had a distinct role in regard to believers in Christ, namely, to promote their holiness: to intercede with the Father when the human mind cannot pray, to turn the mind and imagination to the things of God, and to assist the faithful in understanding spiritual truth and avoiding falsehood (Burgess, 75).

The Holy Spirit continues to give spiritual gifts to believers, although not with the same frequency as in the first century:

The Holy Spirit gave signs of His presence at the beginning of Christ's ministry, and after His ascension He gave still more; but since that time these signs have diminished, although there are still traces of His presence in a few who have had their souls purified by the Gospel, and their actions regulated by its influence. (Burgess, 76)

One of the purposes of such gifts, according to Origen, is to examine and clarify the teachings of the apostles—especially by those who have obtained the gifts of language, wisdom, and knowledge from the Holy Spirit. Another function of the gifts, "signs and wonders," "manifestations of the Spirit and of power," is to validate the teachings of those who perform them, and strengthen the faith of those who observe them (Burgess, 77).

When writing on prayer, Origen began by saying that "what is impossible for human nature becomes possible by the grace of God and the assistance of Christ and the Holy Ghost. Such is the case with prayer." Treating of prayer as adoration, he remarked that such prayer should be directed to God the Father only. "Christ Himself taught us to adore the Father. We should pray in the name of Jesus. We should adore the Father through the Son and in the Holy Ghost, but only the Father is entitled to accept adoration." He concluded by writing that "prayer remains a gift of the Holy Spirit, who prays in us and leads us in prayer" (Quasten II, 66–67, 69).

Origen's writings were not always consistent, and some would later be repudiated, but his search for understanding was quite sophisticated.

Novatian

Novatian was a very prominent priest in Rome when Cornelius was elected pope in 251 and showed inclinations to be lenient and willing to reconcile the *lapsi*, those who fell away from the faith under the imperial persecutions. Novatian took the rigorist position that such persons should not be reconciled with the church but could only receive God's mercy in the next life. He had himself ordained a bishop, became a schismatic, and is considered to be an antipope from 251 to his death in 258. However, Novatian was a brilliant theologian who wrote an outstanding work on the Trinity in 235, when he was in very good standing with the church.

It was in this work that he wrote about the Holy Spirit as subordinate to the Son. As the Son is less than the Father, so the Holy Spirit is less than the Son, he said. He did not call the Holy Spirit the third person, but he did refer to the Son as the second person.

The Holy Spirit was with both the prophets of the Old Testament and the apostles in the New Testament, but in different ways: in the prophets the Spirit was with them only in particular situations, but he abided always in the apostles, poured forth in the Spirit's entirety, through Christ's resurrection. He could not have left them forsaken, without anyone to be their advocate and guardian.

> For it was He Who strengthened their souls and minds, Who clearly brought out for them the mysteries of the gospel, Who threw light within them upon divine things, by Whom they were made strong to fear neither bonds nor imprisonment for the name of the Lord. . . . They were ready-armed and fortified through Him, since they possessed within themselves the gifts which this same Spirit distributes and assigns, like ornaments to the Church, the Bride of Christ.
>
> He it is Who appoints the prophets in the Church, instructs the teachers, distributes the tongues, performs acts of power and of healing, works miracles, bestows the discerning of spirits, assigns governments, suggests counsels, and sets in their right places and due order all other gifts of grace.
>
> In Christ alone He dwelt fully and entirely, . . . but in all his overflowing abundance dispensed and sent forth, so that the rest of mankind can enjoy what I will call a first sip of grace, issuing from Christ. For the source of the Holy Spirit in the entirety of His being ever remains in Christ, in order that from Him might issue streams of gifts and works, because the Holy Spirit dwells in Him in rich affluence. (Quasten II, 230–31)

Novatian wrote that the Holy Spirit brings about our new birth in baptism:

> He is it Who brings about the second birth, from water. Thus He is, as it were, the seed of divine generation, the consecrator of a heavenly birth, the pledge of the promised inheritance, the written bond, so to speak, of eternal salvation, to make us the temple of God and perfect us as His

home. . . . He is given us to dwell in our bodies, and to bring about our sanctification. (Quasten II, 231–32)

Hippolytus of Rome

Hippolytus was born in the latter part of the second century and educated somewhere in a Greek-speaking part of the Roman Empire, perhaps Alexandria. He migrated to Rome early in the third century. When Pope Callistus relaxed the treatment of penitents who had committed serious sins, Hippolytus accused him of leniency and of departing from the tradition of the primitive church. Hippolytus was elected bishop of Rome by a small band of followers and thus became the first antipope. However, he died a martyr in 235 and has been honored as a saint in the church ever since. He was a disciple of Irenaeus, wrote in Greek, and was a prolific author. (Many of his works have been lost, partly because of his schism and erroneous teachings, and partly because Greek became less known in Rome.)

Among the most important of Hippolytus's contributions was the *Apostolic Tradition*, a book of church order containing sacramental and other rituals, prayers and religious practices, written about 215, and reflecting the liturgical life of the church in Rome in the late second century.

The Holy Spirit was invoked in key points in these rituals; for instance, in the consecration of bishops. After being chosen by priests and people, all the neighboring bishops laid their hands on the one elected. All are to keep silent, praying for the descent of the Holy Spirit:

> Then one of the bishops present shall, at the request of all, impose his hand on the one who is being ordained bishop, and shall pray thus, saying: "God and Father of our Lord Jesus Christ . . . pour forth now that power that comes from you, from your Royal Spirit, which you gave to your beloved Son and which He bestowed upon His holy apostles, who established in every place the Church of your sanctification, for the glory and unceasing praise of your name. . . . grant to this your servant . . . by the Spirit of

the high-priesthood to have the authority to forgive sins, in accord with your command.

And after the offering of bread and wine, the presiding bishop continues:

And we pray that you might send your Holy Spirit upon the offering of the holy Church. Gather as one in the fullness of the Holy Spirit your saints who participate; and confirm their faith in truth so that we may praise and glorify you through your Son Jesus Christ, through whom be glory and honor to you, to the Father and the Son with the Holy Spirit, in your holy Church, both now and through the ages of ages. (Jurgens I, 167)

Likewise, Hippolytus reported that the Holy Spirit was invoked also when a presbyter was ordained. The bishop, imposing his hand on the one being ordained, prays:

God and Father of our Lord Jesus Christ, look upon your servant and grant him the Spirit of grace and the counsel of a presbyter, so that he may support and govern your people with a pure heart, as also you looked upon your chosen people and commanded Moses to choose presbyters, whom you filled with your Spirit, which you gave to your servant. And now, O Lord, grant that there may ever be preserved among us the Spirit of your grace, and make us worthy that, in faith, we may give praise to you and minister to you in simplicity of heart: through your Son Jesus Christ, through whom be glory and honor to you, the Father and the Son with the Holy Spirit, in your holy Church, both now and through the ages of ages. (Jurgens I, 167–68)

When a bishop ordained a deacon, he asked, "Grant the Holy Spirit of grace and care and diligence to this your servant, whom you have chosen to serve the Church" (Jurgens I, 168).

Hippolytus described the baptismal ritual in fine detail. It included the Holy Spirit as the object of belief in the profession of faith and was invoked three times in the trinitarian formula, but especially in the rite of confirmation (or chrismation). The bishop lays his hand upon the newly baptized, saying:

> O Lord God, who didst count these Thy servants worthy of deserving the forgiveness of sins by the laver of regeneration, make them worthy to be filled with the Holy Spirit and send upon them Thy grace, that they may serve Thee according to Thy will; for to Thee is the glory, to the Father and to the Son with the Holy Ghost in the holy Church, both now and ever and world without end.
>
> After this, pouring the consecrated oil from his hand and laying his hand on his head, he shall say: I anoint thee with holy oil in God the Father Almighty and Christ Jesus and the Holy Ghost. (Quasten II, 192)

Hippolytus also drew attention in *Apostolic Tradition* to the operation of the gifts of the Spirit in the church, especially the gifts of healing and teaching (Burgess, 83).

Cyprian of Carthage

Cyprian was born between 200 and 210, in or near Carthage, to a wealthy and well-educated pagan family. He gained great fame as an expert rhetorician, and then, reacting to the immorality of both private and public life, and responding to grace, he converted to Christianity (in about 246) and gave his fortune to the poor. Before long he was ordained a priest, and in short order he was elected bishop of Carthage (about 249). He was a devoted follower of Tertullian and was the leader of the church in North Africa. Cyprian was embroiled in the dispute over the *lapsi*, those who had fallen away under the persecutions and later sought to be reconciled. He was beheaded in the persecution of Emperor Valerian in 258.

Cyprian spoke of his own experience of the Holy Spirit at his baptism:

> I was entangled in the thousand errors of my previous life; I did not think that I could get free of them, for I was so much a slave of my vices, . . . and I had such complaisance in the evils which has become my constant companions.

> But the generating water washed me from the stains of my previous life, and a light from on high shone into my heart thus purified from its corruptions, and the Spirit coming from heaven changed me into a new man by a second birth. (Quasten II, 246)

In one of his letters on the issue of the rebaptism of heretics, Cyprian invoked the example of the apostles Peter and John when they encountered the newly baptized Christians in Samaria and found that they had not yet received the Holy Spirit (Acts 8:14–17). The apostles did not rebaptize the Samaritans; instead they prayed that they might receive the Holy Spirit and laid hands on them, and then they received the Holy Spirit. Cyprian wrote to one of his fellow bishops:

> For this reason, then, that they had already received legitimate and ecclesiastical baptism, it was not necessary to baptize them again. Rather, that only that was lacking was done by Peter and John; and thus, prayer having been made over them, and hands having been imposed upon them, the Holy Spirit was invoked and poured out upon them. This is even now the practice among us, so that those who are baptized in the Church are then brought to the prelates of the Church; and through our prayer and the imposition of hands, they receive the Holy Spirit and are perfected with the seal of the Lord. (Jurgens II, 237)

In the same letter Cyprian explained the contradictions involved in heretical baptism:

> If someone could be baptized by heretics, he could also receive the remission of sins. If he were to receive the remission of sins, he would be sanctified. If he were sanctified, he would be made a temple of God. If he were made a temple of God—now I ask you, of what God? Of the Creator? But that is not possible because he does not believe in Him. Of Christ? One who denies that Christ is God cannot become His temple. Of the Holy Spirit? Since the Three are One, how were it possible for the Holy Spirit to be reconciled

to him that is an enemy of either the Son or of the Father?
(Jurgens II, 238)

Clearly Cyprian believed that the Holy Spirit was a full partner
in the holy Trinity, that the Three are one God.

The Council of Nicaea and Afterward

Eusebius of Caesarea

Eusebius, frequently called the father of ecclesiastical history, was
fully engaged in the controversies of his time. He was born in
Caesarea in Palestine about 263, educated there, and was elected
as its bishop in 313. He held Emperor Constantine in highest regard and enjoyed the favor of the emperor, delivering panegyrics
on the occasion of the emperor's twentieth and thirtieth years in
office as well as the eulogy on Constantine's death in 337. He
was seated at the emperor's right hand at the Council of Nicaea.
Eusebius was a tireless scholar and author, more productive than
any other of the Greek church fathers, with the exception of
Origen. He died in 339 or 340.

Eusebius became embroiled in the Arian controversy. Arius, a
presbyter in Alexandria, proposed a doctrine regarding the Son's
relationship to the Father that held only the Father was eternal
and "unoriginated." There was a time when the Son did not exist. The Son is a creature of the Father, the first and greatest of
creatures, created out of nothing to serve as an instrument for the
creation of the rest of creation. The Son was clearly subordinate
to the Father. The Son was neither coeternal nor consubstantial
with the Father; in fact, the Son did not have a divine nature or
attributes. (Little was said about the Holy Spirit in this controversy, but clearly the Spirit too would be consigned to a subordinate role.) This teaching became widespread and divisive, not
only in the church but in the Roman Empire. Eusebius had Arian
leanings, and at times had supported the Arian cause.

Eusebius wrote in *Ecclesiastical Theology* that the Son of God
is not of the same essence as the Father, but only a product of the
Father's free will, and the Holy Spirit is not more than a creation

of the Son (Quasten III, 342). He wrote further that the Holy Spirit is different from the Son, for he comes after the Son has departed. He indwells saints whom the Son has redeemed. He sanctifies all he indwells, imparting his gifts to prophets, apostles, and their successors in the church. However, only the Son shares the honor of the Father. The Son alone creates all things that are made, including the Holy Spirit. The Son has dominion over all things, even over the Spirit (Burgess, 102).

In an earlier work, *Preparation for the Gospel*, Eusebius explained his trinitarian hierarchy using this comparison:

> There is one glory of the sun, and another glory of the moon, and another glory of the stars. . . . In this way, therefore, we must think of the order in incorporeal and intelligent Beings also, the unutterable and infinite power of the God of the universe embracing all of them together; and the second place, next to the Father, being held by the power of the Divine Word, at once creative and illuminating. . . . And next after this Being, there is set as in the place of a moon, a third being, the Holy Spirit, whom also they enroll in the first and royal dignity and honor of the primal cause of the universe. . . .
>
> But this Spirit, holding a third rank, supplies those beneath out of the superior powers in Himself, notwithstanding that He also receives from another, that is from the higher and stronger, who, as we said, is second to the most high and unbegotten nature of God the King of all: from whom indeed God the Word is Himself supplied, and drawing as it were from an ever-flowing fountain which pours forth Deity, imparts copiously and ungrudgingly the radiance of His own light to all, and especially to the Holy Spirit Himself, who is closer to Him than all and very near. (Burgess, 103)

Eusebius gave witness to the positive value of the gifts of the Spirit in the church, like prophecy, healing, wisdom, and knowledge. He compared the gifts that enlighten the world to the lightning that accompanies a storm; the Spirit's *charismata* adorn the church. But Eusebius opposed the Montanists, who featured such gifts but exercised them outside the church. He called them false prophets, and inspired by the devil, not the Holy Spirit. His condemnation was not of their gifts, but of their reviling of the church. The unity of the church was a keen concern of Eusebius.

The Council of Nicaea

In 325, Emperor Constantine, who in 313 called for religious tolerance in the empire, then gradually favored Christianity, called the bishops to a great council to be held in the city of Nicaea, just a few miles east of his capital, Constantinople. The purpose of the council was to resolve the debate with the Arians over the nature of Christ, a conflict that was dividing both church and empire. It was a question of Christology within the Trinity. What was the precise relationship between the Jesus Christ, the Son of God, and the Father? The subtext was the use of nonbiblical language (for example, *substance* and *consubstantial*) to define the relationship. The status of the Holy Spirit seems not to have been at issue, and the Spirit was simply affirmed as an object of belief.

The council opened on June 19, 325, in the presence of the emperor and about three hundred bishops from all over the empire (but mostly from the East); it lasted about four weeks. The resulting formula of the creed was signed by all but two or three of the bishops.

> We believe in one God the Father all powerful, maker of all things, both seen and unseen. And in one Lord Jesus Christ, the Son of God, the only-begotten, begotten from the Father, that is from the substance of the Father, God from God, light from light, true God from true God, begotten not made, consubstantial with the Father, through whom all things came to be, both those in heaven and those in earth; for us humans and for our salvation he came down and became incarnate, became human, suffered and rose up on the third day, went up into the heavens, is coming to judge the living and the dead. And [we believe] in the Holy Spirit. (Tanner I, 5)

There followed a brief condemnation of the positions of the Arians, for example, those who say "there once was when he was not."

At the conclusion of the council Constantine urged all of those assembled to observe its decisions:

> Receive then, with all willingness, this truly Divine injunction, and regard it as in truth the gift of God. For whatever is determined in the holy assembly of bishops is to be regarded as indicative of the Divine will. As soon, therefore, as you have communicated these proceedings to all our beloved brethren, you are bound from that time forward to adopt for yourselves, and to enjoin on others the arrangements above mentioned [in addition to the creed, the council adopted twenty canons for disciplinary matters]. (Burgess, 105)

The agreement on a single, authoritative statement of the church's faith had been worked out and agreed to, but the underlying Arian conflict and division did not end for many more years.

Eusebius of Caesarea signed the creed of Nicaea and no longer wrote or spoke in favor of the Arian cause, despite what may have been his personal convictions, both because of his loyalty to the emperor and of his overarching commitment to the unity of the church.

Cyril of Jerusalem

Born in Jerusalem in about 315, Cyril became the city's bishop in 348. He was a defender of the Nicene creedal statement. The Arian controversy raged in the region, and those of the Arian persuasion had Cyril expelled from his diocese three different times between 348 and 378. Each time he returned, and he died there in 386.

Cyril is best known for a series of lectures given in about 350, during Lent and Easter Week, to catechumens preparing for baptism and for the recently baptized: *Catecheses* and *Mystagogical Catecheses*. What has come down to us of this precious treasure is not Cyril's own writing, but what was written down and transcribed by his hearers. The lectures covered the nature of God and the history of salvation but focused on the sacraments of baptism, confirmation, and Eucharist; consequently, he spoke often and deeply about the Holy Spirit.

The Holy Spirit, like the Son, is a sharer in the divinity of the Father, and at the same time, a distinct personality, with distinct personal actions attributed to him. Cyril said:

> It is established that there are various appellations, but one and the same Spirit—the Holy Spirit, living and personally subsisting and always present together with the Father and the Son; not as being spoken or breathed forth from the mouth and lips of the Father and the Son, or diffused into the air; but as a personally existing being, Himself speaking and operating and exercising His dispensation and hallowing, since it is certain that the dispensation of salvation in regard to us which proceeds from the Father and Son and Holy Spirit is indivisible and concordant and one. (Quasten III, 372)

In teaching about baptism, he said:

> Let no one then suppose that Baptism is merely the grace of remission of sins, or further, that of adoption. . . . Nay we know full well, that as it purges our sins, and conveys to us the gift of the Holy Ghost, so also it is the counterpart of Christ's sufferings. (Quasten III, 373)

Cyril reminded his hearers that the baptismal water received its effectiveness from the *epiclesis*, the prayer over the font:

> Do not think of the font as filled with ordinary water, but think rather of the spiritual grace that is given with the water. . . . The ordinary water in the font acquires sanctifying power when it receives the invocation of the Holy Spirit, of Christ and the Father. (Quasten III, 374)

> Since man is of a twofold nature, composed of body and soul, the [baptismal] purification is also twofold. The water cleanses the body, and the Spirit seals the soul. Thus, having our heart sprinkled by the Spirit and our body washed

with pure water, we may draw near to God. When you go down into the water, then, regard not simply the water, but look for salvation through the power of the Holy Spirit. (Jurgens I, 348–49)

The Lord has given a baptism of repentance, so that our chief sins, or rather, all our sins, may be cast off; and so that we may receive the seal of the Holy Spirit, and thereby be made heirs of eternal life. (Jurgens I, 351)

Cyril also spoke of the anointing with chrism after baptism:

But beware of supposing that this is ordinary ointment. For just as the Bread of the Eucharist, after the invocation of the Holy Spirit is simple bread no longer, but the Body of Christ, so also this holy ointment is no longer plain ointment, not, so to speak, common, after the invocation. Rather, it is the gracious gift of Christ; and it is made fit for the imparting of His Godhead by the coming of the Holy Spirit. The ointment is symbolically applied to your forehead and to your other senses; and while your body is anointed with the visible ointment, your soul is sanctified by the Holy and Life-creating Spirit. (Jurgens I, 360)

Cyril's eucharistic teachings emphasized the role of the Holy Spirit in the changing of water and wine into the body and blood of Christ. The calling down of the Holy Spirit upon the oblation by the *epiclesis* is what effects the change.

We call the merciful God to send forth His Holy Spirit upon the gifts lying before Him; that He may make the bread the Body of Christ, and the wine the Blood of Christ; for whatsoever the Holy Ghost has touched is sanctified and changed. (Quasten III, 276)

Cyril also spoke of receiving the Eucharist that has been trans-formed by the Spirit:

After this, the priest says, "Holy things to the holy." The offerings laid out are holy, having received the visitation of the Holy Spirit. And you are holy, having been deemed worthy of the Holy Spirit. The Holy Things, therefore, correspond to the holy persons. . . . We too are holy, but not by nature; rather, by participation and discipline and prayer. (Jurgens I, 365)

At one point Cyril comments on the meanings of faith:

As a noun the word *faith* is one; yet its meaning is twofold. There is the one kind, dogmatic faith, involving assent of the soul to something or other; and it is profitable to the soul. . . .

But there is a second kind of faith, which is given by Christ as a kind of grace. "For to one is given through the Spirit a word of wisdom; but to another a word of knowledge through the same Spirit; and to another faith, in the same Spirit; and to another, gifts of healing" (1 Cor 12:8–9). This faith, then, which is given as a gift from the Spirit, is not solely doctrinal, but also, it performs works beyond the power of man. (Jurgens I, 352)

Cyril spoke of the *charismata* (gifts of the Spirit), which are distributed quite broadly, to lay persons, to the ordained, to thousands of persons, near and far, all over the known world.

Finally, Cyril, stated clearly that the work of human salvation is the collaborative effort of all three persons of the Trinity:

The Father gives to the Son, and the Son shares with the Holy Spirit For it is Jesus Himself, not I, who says, "Everything is delivered to Me by My Father" (Mt 11, 27); and of the Holy Spirit, He says, "When He, the Spirit of Truth, shall come . . . He shall glorify Me; for He shall receive of what is Mine, and shall announce it to you" (Jn 16:13–14). The Father through the Son with the Holy Spirit gives every gift. The gifts of the Father are not this, and those of the Son that, and of the Holy Spirit the other. For there is one salvation, one power, and one faith. There is one God, the Father; one Lord, His only-begotten Son; and one Holy Spirit, the Advocate, and it is enough for us to know these things. . . . It is sufficient for us, in regard to our salvation, to know that there is a Father, Son, and Holy Spirit. (Jurgens I, 357)

Didymus the Blind

Didymus lived in and around Alexandria for his whole life, from 313 to 398. He lost his sight at the age of four, but in spite of that he became one of the most learned men and prolific authors of his time. Athanasius placed him at the head of the famous catechetical school in Alexandria. Jerome, one of his students, referred to Didymus as his *magister* (teacher). Many of Didymus's writings have been lost, partly because of his defense of Origen and his subsequent condemnation for that reason by the Council of Constantinople in 553.

Sometime before 381 Didymus wrote a treatise on the Holy Spirit that is considered to be the best monograph on the subject in the fourth century. Didymus has been called the theologian of the Holy Spirit. Ambrose used Didymus's work in his own treatise on the Holy Spirit, written in 381. In his work Didymus proved that the Holy Spirit was not a creature but consubstantial with the Father and the Son. From that he concluded that there can only be one operation of the three divine persons:

> It is proved that in all things there is one same operation of the Father, the Son, and the Holy Ghost. There is but one operation where there is but one substance, because whatever are *homoousia* (identical in substance) with the same substance, have likewise the same operations.

On the other hand, Didymus argued from the unity of operation to the unity of nature:

> Since, therefore these *homoousia* are worthy of the same honor and have the same operation, they have the same nature, and do not differ from one another either in divinity or in operation: they alone can exist together, be placed together in the same grade of dignity, and be everywhere be understood with Him Who is one. (Quasten III, 93)

Whoever communicates with the Holy Ghost, communicates immediately with the Father and the Son, and whoever shares in the glory of the Father has this glory from the Son, contributed through the Holy Spirit. So it is proved that in everything there is one same operation for the Father, the Son, and the Holy Ghost. . . .

For when anyone has received the grace of the Holy Ghost, he will have it as a gift from the Father and our Lord Jesus Christ. By one same grace, however, which is from the Father and the Son, completed by the operation of the Holy Spirit, is proved the Trinity of one substance. (Quasten III, 94)

Didymus considered the work of the sanctification of the soul as belonging in some particular way to the Holy Spirit; he was convinced that the Holy Spirit renews us in baptism. His operation is as the "Finger of God," stamping the divine image on the human soul. The Spirit is the plenitude of all gifts, the culminating point of all God's gifts to humankind (Quasten III, 96). He is the first gift, for he is love, and love is the reason for all divine gifts (Burgess, 114).

Didymus reflected on the presence and expanse of the Holy Spirit:

Nothing created can fill the whole world, nor contain all things and be in all things. On the contrary, even for intellectual Powers there is a boundary and a defined quantity. To fill all and contain all and be in all are properties only of the Godhead. But the Holy Spirit's majesty, perpetuity, limitlessness, His being everywhere, through all and in all, is forever. He does indeed fill the world and subsists divinely, and is unrestricted as to power, measuring indeed, but not being measured. (Jurgens II, 62)

The Paraclete, wrote Didymus, contains all the properties of God. He fills all things, He creates, He remits sins, He inspires, and He commands. The operations of all three members of the Trinity must be common and undivided because this is their nature. For example, the incarnation involves the undivided operation of all persons in the Godhead. The same is true of justification and sanctifying grace (Burgess, 115).

Athanasius

A steadfast defender of the faith of Nicaea against the Arians, Athanasius, the most outstanding of the bishops of Alexandria, was born (about 295) and educated in that city. He became bishop in 338, was forced into exile five times for a total of seventeen years, but died in his see in 373. Despite the turbulent disruptions to his episcopal ministry, Athanasius was a prodigious author, skilled in argumentation and explanation. He is often referred to as a pillar of the church.

In about 359 Athanasius wrote a treatise on the Holy Spirit in the form of four letters to Serapion, the bishop of Thmuis (also in exile at the time). The question of the divinity of the Holy Spirit was closely connected to the relationship between the Father and the Son in the Arian controversy. The Arians held that the Son and Holy Spirit were not truly God, but rather creatures of the Father; the Holy Spirit was a ministering spirit, little more than an angel.

Athanasius was very clear that all three persons of the Trinity were truly God:

> There is then a Triad, holy and complete, confessed to be God, in Father, Son and Holy Spirit, having nothing foreign or external mixed with it, not composed of one that creates and one that is originated, but all creative; and it is consistent, and in nature indivisible, and its activity is one. The Father does all things through the Word in the Holy Spirit. Thus the unity of the holy Triad is preserved. Thus one God is preached in the Church, "who is over all (Ephes 4:6), and through all and in all"—"over all" as Father, as beginning, as fountain; "through all" through the Word; "in all" in the Holy Spirit. It is a Triad not only in name and form of the speech, but in truth and actuality. (Quasten III, 67)

The divinity of the Holy Spirit is also demonstrated by the fact that the Spirit deifies those in whom he dwells:

If by participation in the Spirit, we are made "sharers in the divine nature" (2 Pet 1:4), we should be mad to say, that the Spirit has a created nature and not the nature of God. For it is on this account that those in whom He is are made divine. If He makes men divine, it is not to be doubted that His nature is of God. (Quasten III, 76)

Athanasius clearly stated that the Holy Spirit proceeds from the Father. He nowhere said explicitly that the Spirit proceeds from the Son as well, but it seems to be a necessary corollary of his argument; in other words, he implied that the Spirit proceeds from the Son as well as from the Father (Quasten III, 77). The Spirit is the instrument of the Son in both creation and sanctification. From the Son the Spirit receives his mission to create, to sanctify, and to make divine. In addition to his arguments for the full divinity of the Holy Spirit based on his functions and on his relationship with the Son, Athanasius also argues his case upon the Spirit's place within the Trinity. In every activity involving the Spirit, it is the Trinity that acts. The Father and the Son are acting with the Spirit (Burgess, 118–19).

Indeed, as the saying has it, the Godhead is not brought into proof with words, but into faith and reverence in the company of prudent reasoning. . . . Just as the Son is the only-begotten, so also the Spirit, given and sent by the Son, is one and not many, nor is He one comprised of many, but He alone is the Spirit; for, since the Son, the living Word, is one, so also must His sanctifying, enlightening and life-giving Gift be one, perfect and complete—the gift who is said to proceed from the Father, because He shines forth from and is sent from and is given by the Word, who is confessedly from the Father. (Jurgens I, 335)

When the Seraphim glorify God, saying thrice, "Holy, holy, holy Lord Sabaoth," they are glorifying Father, Son, and Holy Spirit. And likewise, just as we are baptized in the name of the Father, and of the Son, so also in the name of the Holy Spirit; and we are made sons of God, not of gods. For it is Father, Son, and Holy Spirit who is Lord of hosts. For the Godhead is one, and there is one God in three Persons. (Jurgens I, 340)

Those who defame the Spirit and call him creature, . . . they ought to be ashamed. If they allow that there is a Trinity, and that they have faith in the Trinity, then let them say whether the Trinity always was, or whether there was a time when the Trinity was not. Indeed, if the Trinity is eternal, the Spirit is not a creature, because he co-exists eternally with the Word and in Him. . . .

For just as the Son, being eternal, is not a creature, so also the Trinity is eternal, and there is no creature in It; and therefore the Spirit is not a creature. As it ever was, so it is even now. And as now It is, so always It was. It is a Trinity, and in It are Father and Son and Holy Spirit. And there is one God, Father over all and through all and in all, who is blessed unto the ages. Amen. (Jurgens I, 337)

Athanasius developed his doctrine of the Spirit around the central issue of salvation. "To deny the Spirit is to deny the very Agent of grace Who has been provided by the Father through the Son to sinful mankind" (Burgess, 120).

John Chrysostom

Born sometime between 344 and 354 in Antioch to a wealthy Christian family, John was educated by his mother, Anthusa, whose husband died when John was an infant, and later by the exceptional scholars of the Antioch school. He lived as a hermit in the nearby mountains for six years before returning to Antioch and being ordained a deacon in 381 and a priest in 386. For twelve years he was charged with the special duty of preaching in the principal church of the city. He did so with such success that he is considered the greatest of Christian pulpit orators and was given the name *Chrysostom* (golden mouth). This blessed period of his ministry ended in 398 when he was consecrated as patriarch of Constantinople, the imperial capital, a city of rivalries and intrigues. He was thrust into a maelstrom of conflicts for which he was not temperamentally suited. His enemies coalesced against him, and he was exiled to Armenia in 404; he died in the wilderness in 407. Emperor Theodosius II, the son of the empress who expelled John, went out to meet John's funeral train when his body was returned to Constantinople in 438, amid solemn celebration, and asked forgiveness for his mother's persecution of Chrysostom.

John Chrysostom wrote treatises and letters, but the vast majority of his writings were in the form of sermons, hundreds and hundreds of homilies, mainly on biblical subjects.

He touched on the Holy Spirit, but not as a central theme. For example, when speaking of the incomprehensibility of God, he wrote that God is not truly known by any creature, but only by the Son and the Holy Spirit (Jurgens II, 92). When writing of the purifying effects of baptism on our sinful nature, Chrysostom compared the waters of baptism to the fire of a smelting furnace in which God "pours out the grace of the Spirit in place of fire, and then brings us forth renewed and refreshed and with a brightness that rivals the rays of the sun" (Jurgens II, 100).

In another place, Chrysostom wrote that to cast out devils and to effect cures is a work of the Holy Spirit (Jurgens II, 111).

In the first of his homilies on the Acts of the Apostles, Chrysostom said that the book was a little-known part of the scriptures, and that he had chosen it for his subject so that those who do not know it may be drawn to it "and not let such a treasure as this to remain out of sight. For indeed it may profit us no less than even the Gospels, so replete is it with Christian wisdom and sound doctrine, especially in what is said about the Holy Ghost" (Quasten III, 440).

One of Chrysostom's best-known works is his treatise *On the Priesthood*. In it he attributed much of the dignity of the priest to the actions of the Holy Spirit:

> The Paraclete Himself established that ministry. . . . [At the sacrifice of the altar] "the priest stands bringing down not fire [as the prophet Elias did], but the Holy Ghost, and he prays long . . . that grace may descend upon the victim, and through it enflame the souls of all and render them brighter than silver fire-tried." (Quasten III, 474)

In speaking elsewhere of the dignity of priests and the forgiveness of sins, Chrysostom wrote:

The things that are placed in the hands of the priest, it belongs to God alone to give. . . . Neither angel or archangel
is able to do anything in respect to what is given by God;
rather Father, Son, and Holy Spirit manage it all; but the
priest lends his own tongue and presents his own hand.
(Jurgens II, 109)

In other words, the priest plays an instrumental role, but it is
God who forgives sins.

Chrysostom envisaged the Holy Spirit as involved in every
step of God's plan of redemption: inspiring the prophets and
evangelists; cooperating with Mary in the incarnation; revealing
Christ himself; carrying on the works and teachings of Christ;
giving life, knowledge, and holiness (Burgess, 124).

However, Chrysostom insisted that the extraordinary gifts of
the Spirit, like working miracles and speaking in tongues, were
for the first-century church only, not for subsequent ages. Now
it is the fruits of the Spirit (love, joy, peace, patience, kindness,
generosity, faithfulness, gentleness, self-control—Gal 5:22–23)
that are called for, rather than the charismatic gifts of the Spirit.
He championed a moral and loving lifestyle rather than dramatic demonstrations. The Holy Spirit is a source of strength
for everyday living rather than as a source of exceptional gifts
(Burgess, 125–26).

The Cappadocians

Three outstanding theologians living in the region of eastern
Turkey called Cappadocia in the last half of the fourth century
played key roles in the solution of the trinitarian controversies
that wracked the church and the empire. They were Basil the
Great, bishop of Caesarea; his younger brother, Gregory of
Nyssa; and Basil's lifelong friend Gregory of Nazianzus. The
three are called the Cappadocians.

Basil the Great

Basil was born about 330 in a wealthy and distinguished family. His mother, Emmelia, the daughter of a martyr, gave birth

to ten children, three of whom became bishops, and her eldest daughter was a model of the ascetic life. All four are honored as saints. Basil was educated by his father, a famous rhetorician, in the schools of Caesarea, Constantinople, and Athens. (It was in Athens that he became fast friends with Gregory of Nazianzus.) He returned to Caesarea in 356 and began a teaching career, but he soon renounced it to embrace a life devoted entirely to God. He journeyed through the Near East in search of a spiritual guide and was inspired by the ascetics he encountered.

He returned to the region of Caesarea, gave his fortune to the poor, and withdrew to a solitary life on the River Iris. However, he was soon joined by others and, before long, had founded a series of monasteries. About 364, Eusebius, the metropolitan of Caesarea, invited him to become a priest and to assist him in leading the local church in his declining years. Eusebius died in 370, and Basil was elected to succeed him as bishop of Caesarea and metropolitan of all of Cappadocia. He founded many hospitals, homes for the poor, and hospices for travelers while constantly fighting against empire-supported Arianism. He defied Emperor Valens's decree banishing him from his see, and eventually the emperor withdrew it.

Basil died in 379, scarcely fifty years of age, but his energetic labors and excellent writings laid the groundwork for the Council of Constantinople in 381, by which Emperor Theodosius brought order and unity to the church.

Basil was a prolific writer, in several forms—theological and liturgical treatises, sermons, and letters—all in very polished style. Perhaps his best-known work is the treatise *On the Holy Spirit*, written in about 375, in which he defends the consubstantiality of the Son and Holy Spirit with the Father. All three are of the same nature and deserve the same honor. The astonishing fact is that Basil, who became known as the doctor of the Holy Spirit, never called the Holy Spirit "God" anywhere in this profound treatise. So fraught was the tension with the Arians that every word about the Trinity had to be carefully weighed. Instead of simply declaring that the Holy Spirit is God, Basil implied, inferred, and even proved the divinity of the Spirit, but without declaring it explicitly. Gregory of Nazianus defended Basil's reticence in this matter:

The enemies [Arians] were on the watch for the unqualified statement "the Spirit is God," which, although it is true, they . . . imagined to be impious; so that they might banish him and his power of theological instruction from the city and themselves be able to seize upon the Church, and make it the starting point and citadel, from which they could overrun with their evil doctrine the rest of the world. Accordingly, by the use of other terms, and by statements which unmistakably had the same meaning, and by arguments necessarily leading to this conclusion, he so overpowered his antagonists that they were left without reply.

That he, no less than any other, acknowledged that the Spirit is God, is plain from his often having preached this truth, whenever opportunity offered, and eagerly confessed it when questioned in private. But he made it more clear in his conversations with me. (Quasten III, 231)

Basil's cautious reticence about declaring the divinity of the Spirit was motivated by his strong desire to reconcile the Arians or at least the semi-Arians to the church.

Basil argued the divine nature of the Holy Spirit from the similarity of its operations to those of the Father and the Son:

We are of necessity guided in the investigation of the divine nature by its operations. Suppose we observe the operations of the Father, of the Son, and of the Holy Ghost to be different from one another, we shall then conjecture, from the diversity of operations, that the operating natures are also different. For it is impossible that things which are distinct, as regards their nature, should be associated as regards the form of their operations: fire does not freeze, ice does not warm; difference of nature implies difference of the operations proceeding from them. Grant then that we perceive the operation of the Father, Son and Holy Ghost to be one and the same, in no respect showing difference or variation; from this identity of operation we necessarily infer the unity of nature. . . . Identity of operation in the case of the Father and of the Son and of the Holy Ghost clearly proves invariability of nature. It follows that . . . the community of essence proves that this title [of God] is very properly applied to the Holy Spirit. (Quasten III, 232–33)

In another place Basil wrote this statement about the relationships and functions within the Trinity:

You have professed your faith in Father, Son and Holy Ghost. Do not abandon this deposit; the Father,—the origin of all; the Son,—only begotten of Him, very God, Perfect of Perfect, living image, showing the whole Father in Himself; the Holy Ghost, having his subsistence of God, the fount of holiness, power that gives life, grace that makes perfect, through Whom man is adopted, and the mortal made immortal, conjoined with the Father and the Son in all things in glory and eternity, in power and kingdom, in sovereignty and godhead, as is testified by the tradition of the baptism of salvation. (Burgess, 135–36)

Basil's great contribution to the doctrine of the Trinity was his insistence on the meanings of *ousia*—the essence or substantial entity of God, common to all three Persons—and *hypostasis*—the existence in a particular mode, the manner of being of each of the Persons. "One nature, three persons" became the universally accepted formula for the Trinity. He wrote:

Ousia has the same relation to *hypostasis* as the common has to the particular. Every one of us shares in existence by the common term *ousia* and is such and such a one by his own properties. In the same manner, in the matter in question, the term *ousia* is common, like goodness or Godhead or any similar attribute, while *hypostasis* is contemplated in the special property of Fatherhood, Sonship, or the power to sanctify. (Quasten III, 229)

It was this position, supported by the other two Cappadocians, Gregory of Nyssa and Gregory of Nazianzus, and backed by the emperor, that carried the day at the Council of Constantinople in 381.

Like most of the other Greek fathers, Basil taught that the Holy Spirit proceeds from the Father through the Son. Rather, the Spirit comes from the Father, but not by generation like the Son, rather He is the breath of the Father's mouth, "the natural goodness and the inherent holiness and the royal dignity extended from the Father through the Only-Begotten to the Spirit" (Quasten III, 233). The Holy Spirit is in some sense *through* the Son and proceeds from him.

Basil taught that the Spirit is the conductor of the symphony of creation and the creator of the church, which fulfills its role through the Spirit in the sanctification of creation. The church is the body of Christ and the fellowship of the Holy Spirit, a community of love ruled and inspired by the Spirit. The Spirit indwells the church as its soul, as Christ is its head.

The church is the assembly of all those the Holy Spirit calls from all nations of the world through the prophets and apostles, and those endowed with the charisms of word and teaching. The church grows and expands as the Paraclete operates in its midst through the instrumentality of those endowed with its charisms. Basil defined charisms as gifts from the Holy Spirit bestowed and accepted for the benefit of others. He also said that all Christians are recipients of the charism of love, the highest of all the gifts of the Spirit, the sum of all of human obligations toward God and neighbors (Burgess, 139–40, 143).

Basil himself was regarded as a *pneumatophor* (spirit bearer), an active receptacle, carrier, and distributor of the Holy Spirit and its charisms (Burgess, 141).

Gregory of Nyssa

Gregory was born into the same distinguished family as Basil the Great in about 335; he was Basil's younger brother. He married but later joined one of Basil's monasteries on the River Iris and was consecrated bishop of Nyssa in 371, at Basil's insistence. Although not particularly adept at ecclesiastical administration, he excelled his older brother in theological depth and sophistication, as well as in literary versatility. He was deposed by his Arian enemies in 376 but reinstated in 378, after the death of Emperor Valens. He played a prominent role in the Council of Constantinople in 381, subsequently preached at imperial funerals there, and died in 394. His writings are extensive, varied, and original.

Gregory spoke of the Trinity in the following terms:

The characteristic of the Father's Person cannot be transferred to the Son or the Spirit, nor on the other hand, can
that of the Son be accommodated to one of the others, or
the property of the Spirit be attributed to the Father and
the Son. But the incommunicable distinction of properties
is considered in the common nature. It is the characteristic
of the Father to exist without cause. This does not apply
to the Son and the Spirit. (Quasten III, 267)

The Persons of the Godhead are separated from one another
neither in time, in place, nor will, nor practice, nor operation,
nor passivity, nor any of the like things such as perceived
with men, but only that the Father is Father and not the Son,
and the Son is Son and not the Father, and likewise the Holy
Spirit is neither Father nor Son. (Jurgens II, 51)

Through the Son and with the Father . . . the Holy Spirit
is also perceived conjointly. The Spirit is not later than
the Son in His existence, as if the Only-begotten could be
thought of as ever having been without the Spirit. Rather,
since the Spirit is from the God of all things, He has for
the cause of His being that from which the Only-begotten
is Light, through which True Light He shines forth. Neither on the grounds of duration nor by reason of an alien
nature can He be separated from the Father or from the
Only-begotten. (Jurgens II, 52)

Gregory clearly distinguished each of the three persons while
maintaining their single divine nature.

He shared the conviction of other Greek fathers that the Holy
Spirit proceeded from the Father through the Son, immediately
from the Son and immediately from the Father. So he taught that
the Spirit was divine and of the same substance as the Father and
Son but also had distinct relationships with both (Quasten III,
287).

Gregory made clear that their activity *ad extra* is one and in
common:

> In the case of the Divine nature we do not . . . learn that
> the Father does anything by Himself in which the Son does
> not work conjointly, or again that the Son has any special
> operation apart from the Holy Spirit; but every operation
> extends from God to the creation, and is named according
> to our variable conceptions of it, has its origin from the
> Father, and proceeds through the Son, and is perfected in
> the Holy Spirit. (Quasten III, 286)

Gregory defended the divinity of the Son and the Holy Spirit
in a sermon entitled "On the Divinity of the Son and the Holy
Spirit." In another discourse he spoke of the divinity of the Spirit
and against those who denied it, the *Pneumatomachoi* (contend-
ers against the Spirit).

He looked upon the sacraments as a continuation of Christ's
incarnation, by which the grace of redemption reaches humankind. It is the Holy Spirit who transforms the material elements
of the sacraments—for example, water, oil, bread, wine—into
fruitful and effective sources of grace. At baptism it is the personal intervention of the Holy Spirit, in addition to water and
faith, that effects the regeneration of the individual. Baptism not
only imparts grace to believers but opens the door to a life in
the Spirit, an augmenting and growth into Christian adulthood.
In the Eucharist, which Gregory referred to as "the table of the
Spirit," it is the Holy Spirit who blesses and sanctifies the material elements, transforming them into the body and blood of
Christ (Burgess, 148).

When compared with the other two Cappadocians, Basil and
Gregory Nazianzus, Gregory was theologically superior. He did
more than defend the faith, he articulated the first systematic pre-
sentation of the whole range of the Christian faith since Origen.

Gregory of Nazianzus

Gregory was born about 330 and died about 390 on his family's
estate in Arianzum, in southwestern Cappadocia. He became the
devoted friend of Basil during his years of studies in Caesarea,
Athens, and elsewhere. His father, also named Gregory, was
the bishop of nearby Nazianzus; his son was ordained a priest
(about 362) at the insistence of his father's congregation. Basil,

in an attempt to consolidate his own position as metropolitan of Cappadocia, made Gregory the bishop of the little village of Sasima. Gregory was very reluctant, and he never took possession of the see but remained in Nazianzus, assisting his father. After his father died in 374, Gregory administered the diocese for a short time. A year later he retired to a monastery for a life of contemplation.

Gregory was then urgently called to Constantinople in 379 to become the bishop of the small community there loyal to the teachings and discipline of the Council of Nicaea. That church had been under siege from the Arian emperors and archbishops and was desperately in need of defense and reorganization. Gregory accepted the call, and for two years he led the restoration of the church, mainly by his outstanding preaching. Emperor Theodosius returned all the church properties to the church, and the Council of Constantinople (381), which the emperor convened, recognized Gregory as bishop of the capital. However, when the bishops from Egypt and Macedonia arrived at the council, they objected to his nomination for canonical reasons (that it was against the canons of the church for a bishop to transfer from one diocese to another). Gregory resigned the see in disgust within a few days and returned to Nazianzus and took charge of that diocese until a new bishop was elected in 384. He spent his final years in writing and prayer on the family estate.

Gregory was not a prolific author, but his orations, letters, and poems were of such exceptional depth and elegance that he was known as the Theologian. His most admired compositions were written during his two years as bishop of Constantinople. One of those was devoted to defending the divinity of the Holy Spirit.

The doctrine of the Trinity was a favorite theme of Gregory's. He emphasized the unity and sovereignty of God, on the one hand, and a clear definition of the divine relations, on the other. He wrote, "There is complete identity among the three divine Persons except for the relations of origin." He defined the distinctive character of the Holy Spirit as *procession*, a term that he originated.

The Father is Father and is Unoriginate, for He is of no one, the Son is Son, and is not unoriginate, for He is of the Father. . . . The Holy Ghost is truly Spirit, coming forth from the Father indeed, but not after the manner of the Son, for it is not by generation but by procession, since I must coin a word for the sake of clearness. (Quasten III, 250)

Gregory spoke of the profession of the Trinity as the identifying symbol of his people:

I am not afraid for my little flock, for it is seen at a glance. I know my sheep and mine know me. . . . My sheep hear my word, which I have heard from the oracles of God, which I have learned from the holy fathers. . . . I call them by name and they follow me. . . . They worship the Father and the Son and the Holy Spirit, One Godhead; God the Father, God the Son, God . . . the Holy Spirit. One Nature in Three Personalities, intelligent, perfect, subsisting of themselves, numerically divided, but not divided in their Godhead. (Jurgens II, 34)

Gregory did not hesitate, as Basil did, to give clear and formal expression to the divinity of the Holy Ghost. "Is the Spirit God? Most certainly." He explained the earlier uncertainty about the nature of the Spirit as a part of the order of development in divine revelation of truth:

The Old Testament proclaimed the Father clearly, but the Son more darkly; the New Testament plainly revealed the Son, but only indicated the deity of the Spirit. Now the Holy Spirit lives among us and makes the manifestation of Himself more certain to us. (Quasten III, 251)

The Holy Spirit is truly holy. No other is such, not in the same way; for He is holy not by an acquiring of holiness but because He Himself is Holiness, not more holy at one time and less holy another time; for there is no beginning in time of His being holy, nor will there ever be an end to it. (Jurgens II, 29)

Gregory spoke of the creativity of the Spirit in the formation of the universe:

The Spirit shares with the Son in working both the Creation and the Resurrection, as you may be shown by this Scripture; By the Word of the Lord were the heavens made, and all the power of them by the breath of His Mouth; and this, The Spirit of God that made men, and the Breath of the Almighty that teaches men, and again, You shall send forth Your Spirit and they shall be created, and You shall renew the face of the earth. (Burgess, 156)

The dispensation of the Spirit has begun, Gregory taught, and the Spirit is at work within the believing Christian, giving the gifts of hope and grace in the deifying waters of baptism. "The Spirit assists us in prayer, in fact it is the Spirit *in* whom we worship and *through* whom we pray. . . . The Spirit dwells within us, shows us the Son who takes us to the Father" (Burgess, 154, 157).

Gregory said that all we know about the Spirit has been revealed to us by the scriptures inspired by the Spirit. In his *Oration on Pentecost* he summarized it this way:

The Holy Ghost, then, always existed, and exists, and always will exist. He neither had a beginning, nor will He have an end; but He was everlastingly ranged with and numbered with the Father and the Son. . . . Therefore He was ever being partaken, but not partaking; perfected; sanctifying, not being sanctified, deifying not being deified; Himself ever the same with Himself, and with those with Whom He is ranged; invisible, eternal, incomprehensible, unchangeable, without quality, without quantity, without form, impalpable, self-moving, eternally moving, with free will, self-powerful . . . Life and Lifegiver; Light and Lightgiver; absolute Good, and Spring of Goodness; the right, the Princely Spirit; the Lord, the Sender, the Separator; Builder of His own Temple; leading, working as He wills; distributing His own Gifts, the Spirit of Adoption, of Truth, of Wisdom. (Burgess, 160)

Gregory of Nazianzus gave us the term *procession* for the origin of the Holy Spirit within the Trinity, he clearly affirmed that the Holy Spirit was God, and that the Spirit was a full partner in the creation and ongoing formation of the universe.

Council of Constantinople

In the year 380 the Roman emperors—Gratian in the West and Theodosius in the East—decided to call a council to counter the Arians, to affirm the teachings of the Council of Nicaea, and to decide the legitimacy of the claimants to two major sees, Constantinople and Antioch. Theodosius convoked the Council at Constantinople in 381. One hundred fifty bishops attended, and all of them were from the East (thirty-six bishops of the *Pneumatomachi* persuasion, those who denied the divinity of the Holy Spirit, came, but they were denied admission).

Gregory of Nazianzus presided for a part of the council, with Gregory of Nyssa as the leading theologian. As we have noted, Gregory of Nazianzus was challenged for having transferred from his see in Cappadocia. He resigned from the council and from his office as bishop of Constantinople, and returned to Nazianzus.

The council affirmed the creed of the Council of Nicaea and added the following passage on the Holy Spirit:

> And [we believe] in the Holy Spirit, the Lord, the Giver of life, who proceeds from the Father, who together with the Father and the Son is worshiped and glorified, who spoke through the prophets. (Jurgens I, 399)

These additional words on the Holy Spirit were to refute the Pneumatomachian heresy. They made it clear that the Spirit is divine, of the same substance as the Father, and equally deserving of adoration as the Father and the Son, hence truly God.

The Council of Chalcedon (451), convoked by Emperor Marcian and attended by five hundred to six hundred bishops, explicitly affirmed the Nicene Creed along with the formula added by the Council of Constantinople for the church in the West as well as in the East:

> This wise and saving creed, the gift of divine grace, was sufficient for a perfect understanding and establishment of religion. For its teaching about the Father and the Son and the holy Spirit is complete, and it sets out the Lord's

becoming human to those who faithfully accept it. (Tanner I, 84)

The divinity of the Holy Spirit was finally, officially, and fully confirmed by the church, from this time to the present.

Hilary of Poitiers

Hilary was born into a wealthy pagan family in the city of Poitiers in France in about 315. He received an excellent education, and after studying the scriptures, he converted to the Christian faith. Although he was married, the clergy and people of Poitiers chose him as their bishop in 350. Emperor Constantius II exiled Hilary to Phrygia in Asia Minor in 356 (because of his resistance to Arian influences); while there, he studied the works of the theologians of the East, Athanasius and others. He returned to Poitiers in 359 and vigorously supported the teachings of the Council of Nicea and strongly opposed the Arians. He is credited with the defeat of Arianism in the West after the death of Constantius in 361. Hilary died in about 368.

Hilary's most celebrated work is *On the Trinity*, written while he was in exile. He commented on Jesus's final command to his disciples (Matt 28:19–20):

> Indeed, what is there of the mystery of human salvation that is not therein contained? . . . He commanded them to baptize in the name of the Father, and of the Son, and of the Holy Spirit: that is, in a confession of the Author, and of the Only-begotten, and of the Gift. There is one Author of all; for God the Father, from Whom are all things, is one. And the Only-begotten, Our Lord Jesus Christ, through Whom are all things, is one. And the Spirit, the Gift in all things, is one.
>
> Everything, therefore, is arranged according to its own properties and merits: there is one Power, from Whom are all things; one Offspring, through Whom are all things; one gift of perfect hope. Nor will anything be found lacking in that grand perfection in which there is, in Father and in Son and in Holy Spirit, infinity in the Eternal, form in the Likeness, and enjoyment in the Gift. (Jurgens I, 373–74)

Father, Son, and Holy Spirit together are one God, equal in nature, perfection, and dignity. Hilary then asked why it is necessary to speak of the existence of the Holy Spirit.

> Concerning the Holy Spirit . . . on account of those who do not know Him, it is not possible for me to be silent. However, it is not necessary to speak of Him who must be acknowledged, who is from the Father and the Son, His Sources. Indeed, it is my opinion that there ought to be no discussion about whether He exists. If He is given, if He is received, if He is retained, then obviously He exists. . . . I think, however, that the reason why some remain in ignorance or in doubt about this, is that they see this third name, that by which the Holy Spirit is named, applied frequently also to the Father and to the Son. But there need be no objection to this, for both the Father and Son are spirit and holy. (Jurgens I, 375)

On the subject of the procession of the Spirit within the Trinity, Hilary used the formula *ex Patre per Filium*. The Spirit is from *(ex)* him from whom are all things (the Father), and through *(per)* whom are all things (the Son).

Further on in the same work Hilary attempted to explain the meaning of the indwelling of the Holy Spirit.

> We are all spiritual men, if the Spirit of God is in us. But this Spirit of God is also the Spirit of Christ. And since the Spirit of Christ is in us, the Spirit of Him also who raised Christ from the dead is in us; and He that raised Christ from the dead will vivify our mortal bodies too, on account of His Spirit's dwelling in us. We are vivified therefore, on account of the Spirit of Christ's dwelling in us through Him that raised Christ from the dead. (Jurgens I, 378)

Hilary wrote about the work of the Spirit in sanctifying and enlightening the believer. After quoting Jesus's words (from John 14:16) about the sending of another Advocate, the Spirit of truth, he explained:

These words were spoken to show how multitudes should enter the kingdom of heaven; they contain an assurance of the goodwill of the Giver, and of the mode and terms of the Gift. They tell how, because our feeble minds cannot comprehend the Father or the Son, our faith which find God's incarnation hard of credence shall be illumined by the gift of the Holy Ghost, the Bond of union and the Source of light. (Burgess, 170)

He went on to write about the Holy Spirit as gift to the human soul:

That Gift, which is in Christ, is One, yet offered, and offered fully, to all; denied to none, and given to each according to the measure of his willingness to receive; its stores the richer, the more earnest the desire to earn them. This Gift is with us unto the end of the world, the solace of our waiting, the assurance, by the favors which He bestows, of the hope that shall be ours, the light of our minds, the sun of our souls. (Burgess, 171)

Hilary of Poitiers was a major conduit for theological thought about the Holy Spirit from the East to the West in the mid-fourth century. He was a major source for Augustine, who forged a synthesis of trinitarian doctrine.

Ambrose of Milan

Ambrose was born in Trier, Germany, about 339, into the family of an officer in the Roman army. His father died young, and his widowed mother moved to Rome with her three children. Ambrose studied law and was made consul of Liguria and Emilia in 370, with residence in Milan. Ambrose intervened in the violent dispute between the Arians and Catholics over the election of a new bishop, only to find himself as the choice of both parties even though at the time he was only a catechumen, not yet baptized. He yielded to the pressure of the parties, and was consecrated bishop of Milan in 374, just a week after his baptism.

Ambrose devoted himself to his ministry, first studying some of the leading theologians of the East, like Athanasius, Basil, and Didymus. He was a stout defender of the faith against both Arians and pagans, and he exercised considerable influence in the failing empire. He was a prolific author, in many forms, including poetry and letters, in addition to biblical commentary and theological treatises. He died in Milan in 397.

Ambrose wrote the treatise *On the Holy Spirit* in 381. In it he employed the image of water, borrowed from both the Old and New Testaments, to illustrate the work of the Holy Spirit.

> So, then, the Holy Spirit is the River, and the abundant River . . . This is the great River which flows always and never fails. And not only a river, but one of copious stream and overflowing greatness, as also David said: "The stream of the river makes glad the city of God."
>
> For neither is that city, the heavenly Jerusalem, watered by the channel of any earthly river, but that Holy Spirit, proceeding from the Fount of Life, by a short draught of Whom we are satiated, seems to flow more abundantly among those celestial Thrones, Dominions, Powers, Angels and Archangels, rushing in the full course of the seven virtues of the Spirit. For if a river rising above its banks overflows, how much more does the Spirit, rising above every creature, when He touches the as it were low-lying fields of our minds, make glad that heavenly nature of the creatures with the larger fertility of His sanctification. (Burgess, 173)

The stream proceeding from the living Fount of God is the grace of the Spirit promised by the prophet Joel, "I will pour out my Spirit upon all flesh" (Joel 2:28). He is a river of peace, and it is in the water of baptism that the soul experiences the grace of the life-giving Spirit.

Ambrose was concerned about the nature of the Spirit. He stated that it was the same Spirit who spoke through the prophets and the apostles, and who was called the Spirit of God and of Christ. The Spirit is not a creature, but higher; the Spirit sanctifies both angels and humankind. The Spirit displayed properties showing him to be the equal of the Father and the Son: power, creativity, life, and light. Moreover, the Spirit forgives sin and receives worship and does not offer it. The Holy Spirit is divine, as Jesus witnessed.

The Spirit is one with the Father and the Son in divine operations *ad extra*. The three are united in one Godhead, in one power, and in one counsel, hence they are united in one substance. Yet the Spirit is a separate person, distinct without separation, without confusion, without plurality.

[The Spirit] exists then, and abides always, Who is the Spirit of His [the Father's] mouth, but He seems to come down when we receive Him, that He may dwell in us, that we may not be alien from His grace. To us he seems to come down, not that He does come down, but that our minds ascend to Him. (Burgess, 175)

On the issue of the procession of the Spirit, Ambrose used both the expression "from the Father through the Son," and "from the Father and the Son." (The Latin Church, following Augustine, eventually adopted the latter formula. The Eastern Church maintained the former.)

In the grand scheme of redemption the Spirit operates from the time of creation to the present (fourth century) state of the church. Every creative activity of the Father operates through the Son and receives its fulfillment and completion in the action of the Spirit. The whole universe receives its actuality and perfection through the Spirit, and that which the Spirit creates, the Spirit also renews.

The creative Spirit is also the Giver of revelation, and the Author of the incarnation. He reveals the things of God, the mystery of God's design for redemption. His role in the plan of salvation is fulfilled at Pentecost when he descended with power. The Spirit becomes the primary link binding Christ to the church; the church is built by the Spirit (Burgess, 176).

Life in the Spirit, for Ambrose, began with the sacraments. In baptism, he wrote, the Spirit renews the mind, effects the reality of the new birth, and makes us children by adoption. In confirmation the Spirit seals the soul of the believer and imparts the gifts of wisdom, understanding, counsel, strength, knowledge, godliness, and holy fear. In the Eucharist the Spirit actualizes the mystery of salvation, from the incarnation to the resurrection. In ordination the Spirit provides power to the priest to forgive sins; the office of the priest is a gift of the Holy Spirit.

> Note well that it is through the Holy Spirit that sins are forgiven. Men make use of their ministry in the forgiveness of sins, but they are not exercising any power that is theirs by right. It is not in their own name, but in the name of the Father and of the Son and of the Holy Spirit that they forgive sins. They ask and the divinity forgives. The ministration is of man, but the gift bestowed is from the Power on high. (Jurgens II, 157)

Grace comes to humankind through the agency of the Holy Spirit. All creatures, in fact, depend on the Spirit for sanctification, whether angels, dominions, powers, or humans. The Spirit also illuminates the human mind, and the Spirit leads believers to all truth, to the extent that we are able to receive it.

The Holy Spirit infuses holiness in others, through the Spirit we attain to the image and likeness of God and become partakers of the divine nature.

> Good, then, is the Holy Spirit, but good not as acquiring but as imparting goodness. For the Holy Spirit does not receive from creatures, but is received; as also He is not sanctified, but sanctifies; for the creature is sanctified, but the Holy Spirit sanctifies. In which matter, though the word is used in common, there is a difference in the nature. For both the man who receives and God Who gives sanctity are called holy, as we read, "Be ye holy, for I am holy." Who then can dare to say that the Holy Spirit is separate from the Father and the Son, since through Him we attain to the image and likeness of God, and through Him, as the Apostle Peter says, are partakers of the divine nature? (Burgess, 179)

> How could it be that the Holy Spirit would not have all that pertains to God, seeing that He is named along with the Father and the Son when priests baptize, is invoked in the oblations, is proclaimed along with the Father and the Son by the seraphim in the heavens, dwells with the Father

and Son in saints, is poured out on the just, and is given as the source of inspiration in the prophets? So too all divine Scripture is called divinely inspired, because of the fact that God inspires what the Spirit has spoken. (Jurgens II, 157)

In these and other ways Ambrose argued strongly for the divinity of the Holy Spirit. From a pastoral and sacramental perspective he drew upon the rich imagery of both the Old and New Testaments.

Augustine of Hippo

Augustine was born in 354 in Tagaste, in the Roman Province of Numidia (present-day Algeria), North Africa, to a pagan father and a devoutly Christian mother, Monica. He grew up speaking Latin and went to schools in Tagaste, Madaura, and Carthage. He studied and taught in Carthage from 370 to 383. He became accomplished in speech and communications arts. In this period he embraced Manicheism (a dualism of a good god and an evil god) but renounced it after moving to Rome in 383. During this time Augustine lived with a concubine with whom he had a son, Adeodatus (Godsent). They accompanied him to Rome.

He received an office as court orator that caused him to move to Milan, where he became a Neoplatonist, and was helped by a priest, Simplician, toward his conversion to Catholicism. He attended Bishop Ambrose's pre-baptismal instructions and was baptized by him in 387 on Easter eve. The following year Augustine returned to Tagaste, and then to the seaport town of Hippo to establish a monastery and to prepare for his ordination to the priesthood in 391. He was consecrated as bishop of Hippo in 395. For the next thirty-five years Augustine was tireless in the leadership of his diocese, of the church in North Africa, and constant in his refutation of Donatists, Pelagians, Manicheans, and Arians.

Donatism was a local schism and heresy born out of the persecution of Emperor Diocletian (303–5) in Carthage, during which Christians were targets, and those who compromised were considered traitors to the faith and were refused reconciliation. The Donatists were not a tiny sect, but a large church, widespread and entrenched throughout North Africa. At a conference held in the year 411, 284 Donatist bishops attended compared to 286 Catholic bishops. They were Augustine's constant companions and rivals. Augustine's literary productivity was prodigious, the equivalent of a fifteen-volume encyclopedia in modern terms, and some of his works remain among the classics of Western literature. He died in 430, while Hippo was under siege by the Vandals.

In his writings about the inner life of God, Augustine tended to focus on the relationship among the three equal persons, as over against the Eastern theologians, who concentrated on the ontological unity of the Trinity. Most of the adversaries against whom he wrote denied the full divinity of the Holy Spirit. Augustine wrote that the Holy Spirit is at one and the same time God and the Gift of God. In all three persons the divinity is equal and the unity inseparable. The Spirit is consubstantial and coeternal with the Father and the Son, the communion of divine mutual love between the Father and the Son (Burgess, 180–81).

> The Spirit is both the Spirit of God Who gave Him, and ours who have received Him. . . . The Father and the Son are a Beginning of the Holy Spirit, not two Beginnings; but as the Father and Son are one God, and one Creator, and one Lord relatively to the creature, so are they one Beginning relatively to the Holy Spirit. But the Father, the Son, and the Holy Spirit is one Beginning in respect to the creature, as also one Creator and one God. (Burgess, 181)

> We must now treat of the Holy Spirit, so far as by God's gift is permitted to see Him. And the Holy Spirit, according to the Holy Scriptures, is neither of the Father alone, nor of the Son alone, but of both; and so intimates to us a mutual love, wherewith the Father and the Son reciprocally love one another. (Burgess, 181–82)

Because the Holy Spirit is the Spirit of both the Father and the Son, it follows that the Spirit proceeds from both. Augustine gave definitive shape to this position of the Western church, in contrast to the Eastern church position which teaches that the Spirit proceeds from the Father *through* the Son. He cited the words and gesture of the risen Jesus from the Gospel of John to show that the Spirit came from the Son as well as from the Father.

> "Peace be with you. As the Father has sent me, so I send you." When he had said this he breathed on them and said to them, "Receive the Holy Spirit If you forgive the sins of any, they are forgiven them; if you retain the sins of any, they are retained." (John 20:22)

Augustine used human psychology as an analogy to understand God's actions. In this analysis he compared the Holy Spirit to the human will, enabling humans to obey God's law.

> We . . . affirm that the human will is so divinely aided in the pursuit of righteousness, that . . . he receives the Holy Ghost, by whom there is formed in his mind a delight in, and a love of, that supreme and unchangeable good which is God . . . in order that by this gift to him of this earnest, as it were, of the free gift, he may conceive of an ardent desire to cleave to his Maker, and may burn to enter upon the participation in that true light, that it may go well with him from Him to whom he owes his existence. . . . Now, in order that such a course may engage our affections, God's "love is shed abroad in our hearts," not through the free will which arises from ourselves, but "through the Holy Ghost which is given to us." (Burgess, 183)

In the same vein Augustine called the Spirit the gift of God to aid us morally.

> For truly the same Jesus Christ, the only begotten, that is, the only Son of God our Lord, was born of the Holy Spirit and the Virgin Mary. And certainly the Holy Spirit is the Gift of God, which gift is in truth itself equal to the Giver. For without the Gift of God, that is, without the Holy Spirit, through whom charity is diffused in our hearts, the law can command, but cannot help. (Burgess, 183)

Augustine employed many images to describe the Holy Spirit: fire, from the tongues of fire at Pentecost and Jesus saying that

"I am come to send fire on the earth" (Luke 12:49); streams of water, from the river that makes glad the city of God, and the Fountain from which the Spirit calls believers to drink; the Sword of the Lord; the Creator; the Bread; the Shepherd; the Energizer, who renews our moral faculty; the Teacher, leading humankind to all truth; the Finger of God, reaching out to touch humankind, to inspire biblical writers, and to nourish believers.

The Holy Spirit, Augustine said, reproves the world of sin, and remits sins, with or without the aid of humans, but remission of sins is the gift of the Holy Spirit to the church.

> For outside the Church there is no remission of sins. She received as her very own the pledge of the Holy Spirit, without whom no sin whatever is remitted, so that those to whom sins are remitted receive life everlasting. (Burgess, 185)

Augustine taught that the Spirit-given ability "to speak in other languages" (Acts 2:4), conferred on the disciples as part of the Pentecost event, seen as a harbinger of the worldwide mission of spreading the gospel message to all nations, crossing all language barriers, was no longer experienced because it had been replaced by the presence of the Holy Spirit as "the bond of peace of the Church which is spread throughout all nations." Similarly he thought that the gift of speaking in tongues (1 Cor 12:10; 14:2–40) was a "betokening" of what was to come in the mission of the apostles and disciples, and was given for a time and has now passed away. The church itself now speaks in the tongues of all nations.

Likewise, although he believed in the possibility of miracles, like the exercises of "the gift of healing by the same Spirit" spoken of by Paul (1 Cor 12:9), and even witnessed some himself, Augustine thought that they too had largely ceased, but that there were other forms of the Holy Spirit's active involvement in human affairs (Burgess, 189–92).

Filioque

By the time Augustine died in 430, the basic doctrines about the Holy Spirit and the Spirit's "place" within the Trinity were settled. The Holy Spirit is God, not an angel or a creature of any sort. The Holy Spirit is a full partner in the holy Trinity, eternal and powerful, like the Father and the Son.

All of the Trinity's actions or operations outside itself, *ad extra*, in relation to creation, cosmos, or humankind, are the actions of all three together, operations of the triune God, not of the individual persons: Father, Son, Holy Spirit.

What distinguished the persons one from the other *ad intra*, in their "internal" relationships, were their origins: the Father is Unbegotten, the Son is Only-Begotten, and the Spirit proceeds.

Beyond those basic, agreed-upon teachings, there was one subtle difference between many of the theologians of the East and those of the West: How does the "proceeding" of the Holy Spirit take place? From the Father only? Or from the Father *and* the Son (translated as *Filioque,* "and the Son")? The Easterners held the first position, and many of the Western fathers held the second.

The Council of Constantinople (381) solemnly declared in its creed that the "Holy Spirit . . . proceeds from the Father," and that decision was explicitly affirmed by the Council of Chalcedon (451). It was affirmed yet again at the third Council of Constantinople (680) and the same creed was recited again at the second Council of Nicaea (787). One would think that those formal conciliar endorsements would end the matter. Not so.

Sometime in the sixth century, in Spain, someone inserted the word *(filioque)* in the Nicene-Constantinopolitan creed, "the Holy Spirit . . . proceeds from the Father *and the Son*," in an attempt to counter the Arian claims that neither the Son nor the Spirit are truly divine and equal to the Father. The insertion was validated in a local council in Toledo in 589, and from there it was picked up by the Germans and French and, in the seventh century was accepted in Rome.

What was intended to clarify and strengthen the profession of faith turned into a major point of contention between the churches of East and West. The objection from the Easterners was both jurisdictional and doctrinal. The Westerners, and Rome in particular, had no right to change the officially sanctioned creedal formula unilaterally, without the authorization of a general council. Doctrinally, they alleged that the change upset the balance within the Trinity, making the Spirit subject to the Son and hence undermining the Spirit's role in the plan of salvation.

Emperor Charlemagne (800–814) adopted the insertion of *filioque* in the creed in the Frankish kingdom, but Pope Leo III (795–816), who crowned him emperor, professed belief in the doctrine but refused to insert it into the creed out of respect for the Eastern church and his unwillingness to alienate it.

Patriarchs of Constantinople, Photius (858–63, 877–86) and Michael Cerularius (1043–58) prominent among them, engaged in debate with popes and cardinals over the *filioque* controversy, both citing major theologians from Tertullian, Origen, and Athanasius to Hilary, Basil, and Augustine, and debating the meaning of Jesus's own words about the Spirit in the Gospel of John and elsewhere. Did those words refer to the intra-trinitarian *procession* of the Spirit or to the extra-trinitarian *mission* of the Spirit to the disciples and all of humankind?

The issue continued to fester, amid a welter of other differences, misunderstandings, and resentments between the churches of the East and the West throughout the ninth to eleventh centuries, and climaxed with their mutual excommunications in the year 1054, the cataclysmic event that separated the Western and Eastern churches then and ever since.

Many attempts have been made since the eleventh century to heal this disastrous divide; in fact, two ecumenical councils were largely devoted to this concern. The first was in the late thirteenth century, the second Council of Lyon (1274), convened by Pope Gregory X (1272–76), whose first aim was the reunion of the Eastern and Western churches. It was a gathering of over four hundred bishops, abbots, and theologians. The council succeeded in approving a formula of faith in the Trinity which bridged the divisive issue of the procession of the Holy Spirit:

> We profess faithfully and devotedly that the Holy Spirit proceeds eternally from the Father and the Son, not as from two principles, but as from one principle; not by two spirations, but by one single spiration. This the holy Roman church, mother and mistress of all the faithful, has till now professed, preached and taught; this she firmly holds, preaches, professes, and teaches; this is the unchangeable

and true belief of the orthodox fathers and doctors, Latin and Greek alike. (Tanner I, 314)

The theological statement of *filioque*, that the Spirit did indeed proceed from the Father *and* the Son, was accepted by representatives of both sides, East and West, but to little avail. The agreement of the Easterners may have been coerced by the emperor in Constantinople, Michael VIII (1259–82), for political reasons, and the formula was not acceptable to the clergy and people of the Eastern churches. The reunion of the churches was fleeting and ineffective.

A second major effort at the reunion of the Eastern and Western churches was made in the fifteenth century at a general council convened at Basel by the authority of Pope Martin V (1417–31). Later, the council was transferred to Florence. There, on July 6, 1439, with the blessing of Pope Eugenius IV (1431–47) and John VIII Palaeologus, the emperor, and assent of patriarchs of the East, the council approved a decree of union between the churches, joyfully proclaiming:

> *Let the heavens be glad and let the earth rejoice.* For, the wall that divided the western and eastern church has been removed, peace and harmony have returned, since *the corner-stone, Christ, who made both one*, has joined both sides with a very strong bond of love and peace, uniting and holding together them in a covenant of everlasting unity. (Tanner I, 524)

The decree went on to describe the differences between the two views on the procession of the Holy Spirit and the labor that had gone into their efforts to understand one another and clarify their differences and overcome their misunderstandings. The decree finally declared:

> In the name of the holy Trinity, Father, Son, and holy Spirit, we define, with the approval of this holy universal council of Florence, that the following truth of faith shall be believed and accepted by all Christians and thus shall all profess it: that the holy Spirit is eternally from the Father

and the Son, and has his essence and subsistent being from the Father together with the Son, and proceeds from both eternally as from one principle and a single spiration. We declare that when holy doctors and fathers say that the holy Spirit proceeds from the Father through the Son, this bears the sense that thereby also that the Son should be signified, according to the Greeks indeed as cause, and according to the Latins as principle of the subsistence of the holy Spirit, just like the Father.

We define also that the explanation of those words "and from the Son" was licitly and reasonably added to the creed for the sake of declaring the truth and from immanent need. (Tanner I, 526, 527)

The council repeated this same teaching, at even greater length, in its bull of union with the Copts on February 4, 1442 (Tanner I, 570–71).

Once again the procession of the Holy Spirit from both the Father and the Son *(filioque)* was affirmed in the most solemn manner by a general council. Representatives of both East and West had again reached and expressed their agreement. The council fathers went so far as to justify as lawful and reasonable the insertion of the word *filioque* into the creed, accomplished centuries before, as both in keeping with the truth and necessary for pastoral reasons to resist the Arians.

This theological solution to the centuries-old conflict over the procession of the Holy Spirit within the Trinity, although one of the key issues in the separation of the churches of East and West, did nothing to reunite them. Emperor John VIII had faced a desperate situation. The Ottoman Turkish forces were threatening Constantinople, and he agreed to the *filioque* agreement in the hopes of getting military assistance from the West. The aid was not forthcoming. When the Eastern delegates to the council returned home, they did not proclaim the new agreement until 1452 for fear that the people would reject it, and in 1453 Constantinople fell to the Ottoman Turks, who would control it until the First World War. The Byzantine Empire was ended, and the separation of Eastern Christians from those in the West endures until this day. The Eastern churches still reject the teaching that the Spirit proceeds from the Son.

It was an entirely unexpected turn of events that a dispute about the eternal origin of the Holy Spirit—who has been called "the strong bond, the indivisible love, and the insoluble unity between the Father and the Son," and that it is "through the Holy Spirit which is given to us that God's love is poured out into our hearts"—should be the occasion, at least in part, of the thousand-year alienation and separation of the two largest Christian communities in the world (Pelikan III, 146).

The basic theological portrait of the Holy Spirit was complete by the medieval period. Even the differences between East and West over the procession of the Holy Spirit within the Trinity had been neutralized, at least to the extent that each side could continue to use its own version of the creed without being called heretics by the other side. They had come to realize that, despite their verbal differences, they both implicitly understood the same thing about the Spirit, whether the *filioque* was expressed or not. Thomas Aquinas (1225–74), who died on his way to the Council of Lyon, described it this way: the Greeks themselves understand that the procession of the Holy Spirit is ordered somehow to the Son. They concede that the Holy Spirit is the *Spirit of the Son,* and is from the Father *through the Son* (*Summa Theologiae*, I, q. 36, art. 2).

The outstanding theologians and mystics of the Middle Ages did not so much add substantially to what they had received regarding the Spirit as they did imagine, apply, and speculate about the teachings they accepted from earlier sources. For instance, Richard of St. Victor (d.1173) wrote that in the Trinity the love of the Father and the Son overflows and expresses itself as the Holy Spirit, who is pure charity, and that the Holy Spirit is the creative force in the universe; the whole Trinity operates through the Holy Spirit for both creation and its preservation. The great Franciscan theologian Bonaventure (1217–74) focused on the Spirit's role in *The Soul's Journey into God,* the title of his most famous work. Another example is Catherine of Siena (1347–80), who argued that the church only flourishes to the extent that the Spirit's calls and gifts to each person are recognized and encouraged.

Other notables in the Middle Ages who explored the workings of the Spirit include Bernard of Clairvaux (1090–1153), Hildegard of Bingen (1098–1179), Bridget of Sweden (1302–73), and

Julian of Norwich (1342–1416). But the basic contours of the doctrine of the Holy Spirit had already been established.

This concludes this attempt to trace a history of the Holy Spirit as it was revealed to humankind from the scriptures, the life and ministry of Jesus of Nazareth, the earliest Christian communities, the early councils of the church, and subsequent theologians.

The Holy Spirit, which was explicitly recognized as guiding the early church, continues to be the driving force behind the evolution of the church into the future. The Spirit is the internal dynamic, the engine that propels the Christian communities forward and in converging trajectories. The Spirit should be explicitly acknowledged as such.

The foregoing pages have described the gradually realized understanding about the Holy Spirit, the dynamic force behind the church's development, and the many ways in which the Spirit engages believing individuals and communities.

In the next chapter we turn to the goal or target toward which the church tries to evolve, namely, the reign of God that was at the heart of the preaching of Jesus of Nazareth.

Chapter 3

The Evolutionary Goal:
The Reign of God

Jesus of Nazareth in his life and ministry proclaimed the kingdom of God as his central message. The church, which carries on the mission of Jesus, must have the kingdom of God as its goal toward which it aims and is drawn. We envision it as a powerful attractive force pulling the church's evolution forward toward its destiny. It is beautifully described in the preface for the solemnity of Our Lord Jesus Christ, King of the Universe:

> Holy Father, almighty and eternal God, you anointed your Only Begotten Son, our Lord Jesus Christ . . . as King of all creation, so that . . . he might accomplish the mysteries of human redemption, and, making all created things subject to his rule, he might present to the immensity of your majesty an eternal and universal kingdom, a kingdom of truth and life, a kingdom of holiness and grace, a kingdom of justice, love and peace.

Note that the Lord is addressed as "King of all creation" and that "all created things are subject to his rule," the entirety of the cosmos and the entirety of the church. His kingdom is eternal and universal, and it is characterized by truth, life, holiness, grace, justice, love, and peace.

The reign of God, announced by Jesus, stands before the people of the church as more than a target to aim at; it is more like an immense magnet attracting their energies toward the goal, like a gravitational pull. This great project gives meaning to the church's mission and ministry. The purpose of the church on earth is to point toward and enable God's reign.

The Sayings of Jesus about the Reign of God

There is no doubt that the kingdom of God was a major part of Jesus's preaching. Scholars agree that the reign of God was the central theme of the public proclamation of Jesus. This is indicated by the number of times that Jesus uttered the expressions "kingdom of God" or its equivalents, "kingdom of heaven" and "kingdom of my Father"; in the four Gospels they occur over fifty times. Many, probably most, are considered to be actual sayings of the historical Jesus rather than familiar expressions provided by the evangelists for their narratives.

Some examples of these sayings of Jesus about the reign of God are readily recognized by anyone who has heard or read the Gospels:

- "Your kingdom come" in the Our Father (Matt 6:10; Luke 11:2)
- "Blessed are you who are poor, for yours is the kingdom of God" in the beatitudes (Luke 6:20)
- "Truly, I tell you, among those born of women no one has arisen greater than John the Baptist; yet the least in the kingdom of heaven is greater than he" (Matt 11:11)
- "But if it is by the Spirit of God that I cast out demons, then the kingdom of God has come to you" (Matt 12:28)
- "For, in fact, the kingdom of God is among you" (Luke 17:21)
- "I will never again drink of the fruit of the vine until that day when I drink it new in the kingdom of God" at the last supper (Mark 14:25; Luke 22:18)

This random selection of the sayings of Jesus about the reign of God illustrates the wide range of situations, from the beginning of his public ministry to its end, in which he invoked this theme. It was a dominant motif in his thinking, conversations, and preaching.

It is important to note that this level of usage and emphasis on the reign of God is characteristic of Jesus of Nazareth, and no one else. That is not to infer that Jesus invented the notion. The symbolism of God's kingship and kingdom was found in various books of the Old Testament, especially among the prophets, in Psalms, and in the book of Daniel, but it was not a pervasive and dominant theme in the Old Testament as it was for Jesus.

In addition to the books of the Old Testament, the Jewish religious literature written between the Old and New Testaments, that is, from the beginning of the first century BCE to the middle of the first century CE, were or could have been available to Jesus. (These include the book of Enoch, the book of Jubilees, the Testament of Moses, the Psalms of Solomon, as well as documents from the Qumran community, the Dead Sea Scrolls.) They all spoke of God's kingly rule in one way or another, but for none of them was it the central or dominant theme. However, these sources provided the vocabulary, the imagery, and the symbol that Jesus could have learned from them and chose to develop into the dominant, overarching theme for his own ministry. The notion of God's reign was part and parcel of his religious tradition. He took it and developed it into the central symbol of his ministry.

What Jesus Meant by the Reign of God

The exact expression *kingdom of God* or *reign of God* was extremely rare before it was used by Jesus almost as a slogan for his ministry. The larger concept of God's exercising a powerful rule over creation and over the chosen people was found in some parts of the Old Testament, but not the precise term used repeatedly by Jesus. What did Jesus mean by it?

The reign of God is a "symbol that encapsulates a dynamic event, a whole mythic drama of God coming in power to conquer His enemies and establish his definitive rule in Israel" (Meier II, 11). It is an event, a series of actions that admit of stages, a series of conflicts and victories, but with a final victory yet to come. The reign of God stands for the whole *story* of God's saving actions, for God's powerful rule as king over his people, his creation, and the history of both. It tells of God's actions upon and his relationships with those over whom he rules. It is a dynamic, ongoing happening involving God and God's people, and eventually all of creation.

The reign of God has been called a *tensive* symbol, meaning that it is elastic, flexible; it evokes a whole range of meanings. It might be called *polysemous* (having multiple meanings). It involves a complex reality: God's relations with God's people. It is rich with meaning. Jesus spoke as though he had the notion clear in his mind, but he described it *both* in terms of his ministry, his own present time and actions, *and* the kingdom yet to come, the future, the *eschaton*, the end time. Many authors employ the expression "already and not yet" to explain the relationship between the present, partial realizations of the kingdom and its future fulfillment.

God's Reign as Already Present

Jesus believed, spoke, and acted as though the kingdom had already arrived, at least partially or symbolically, in his own words and actions. He spoke as though God's reign had, in some sense, already begun.

One example occurred at the very beginning of his public ministry when Jesus heard that John the Baptist had been arrested, and he withdrew to Galilee. "From that time Jesus began to proclaim, 'Repent, for the kingdom of heaven has come near'" (Matt 4:17). Jesus echoed the words of John the Baptist (Matt 3:2), but he meant that God's rule was already beginning to be present in his own ministry.

Another illustration of this "alreadyness" of God's reign is in the exchange between the disciples of John the Baptist and Jesus while John was in prison.

> When John heard in prison what the Messiah was doing, he sent word by his disciples and said to him, "Are you the one who is to come, or are we to wait for another?" Jesus answered them, "Go and tell John what you hear and see: the blind receive their sight, the lame walk, the lepers are cleansed, the deaf hear, the dead are raised, and the poor have the good news brought to them. And blessed is anyone who takes no offense at me." (Matt 11:2–6)

Jesus clearly indicated that he was fulfilling the prophecies of Isaiah, "The spirit of the Lord God is upon me, because the Lord has anointed me" (61:1–2). He was doing something new, miracles of healing, proclaiming good news to the poor, in his own ministry. God must be the power behind Jesus's words and actions. God's kingly actions were there for all to see.

A few lines later in Matthew's narrative of this passage about John the Baptist, Jesus named the newness *kingdom*.

> What did you go out to see? A prophet? Yes, I tell you, and more than a prophet. This is the one about whom it is written, "See, I am sending my messenger ahead of you, who will prepare your way before you." Truly I tell you, among those born of women, no one has arisen greater than John the Baptist; yet the least in the kingdom of heaven is greater than he. (Matt 11:9–11)

The contrast between John the Baptist and someone who has just accepted Jesus, his message, and his healing ministry, was a comparison of present realities, not of future promises. John, who was acknowledged and celebrated as a prophet and hero, is lesser than one of Jesus's followers who has "entered into the kingdom" and is "already experiencing God's powerful, redeeming, healing, gladdening rule in his life" (Meier II, 402). That person, a believer in Jesus, is already in the kingdom. The end time is now; the kingdom has arrived and can be experienced in the ministry of Jesus. For that reason the newest follower of Jesus is "better off" than even the great John the Baptist.

Another illustration of the kingdom already present in the ministry of Jesus is found in the exorcisms that he performed, that is, the expulsion of what appeared to be demonic forces from those seen to be possessed by them. Jesus was a first-century Jewish exorcist, and that accounted for much of his fame at the time. Jesus most likely saw his exorcisms as part of his ministry of healing and liberating the people of Israel from the illnesses and other evils that afflicted them. However, what distinguished Jesus from other exorcists of his time was that he combined in one person the role of a moral teacher, leader of disciples, and prophet.

An instance of Jesus's exorcism and his response to the Pharisees who alleged that he drove out demons with the power of Beelzebul is found in the Gospels of Matthew and Luke.

> Then they brought to him a demoniac who was blind and mute; and he cured him, so that the one who had been mute could speak and see. All the crowds were amazed and said, "Can this be the Son of David?" But when the Pharisees heard it, they said, "It is only by Beelzebul, the ruler of the demons, that this fellow casts out the demons." He knew what they were thinking and said to them, "Every kingdom divided against itself is laid waste, and no city or house divided against itself will stand. If Satan casts out Satan, he is divided against himself; how then will his kingdom stand? If I cast out demons by Beelzebul, by whom do your own exorcists cast them out? Therefore they will be your judges. But if it is by the Spirit of God that I cast out demons, then the kingdom of God has come to you." (Matt 12:22–28; Luke 11:14–20)

Jesus tied his exorcism of the Israelite to the coming of God's kingdom at the present time. God's coming in power to manifest his rule in the end time had begun with Jesus's action of expelling the demon by the power of God's Spirit. The troubled demoniac was liberated from the power of demons by the power of God working in Jesus. In this sense the kingdom of God, God's saving rule, had already come to an enslaved Israelite who was liberated by the exorcism and also to those who witnessed this display of God's power and believed in it (Meier II, 414–15).

Another passage from the Gospel of Luke points to the fact that the reign of God is already present in the ministry of Jesus. Again it takes place in a dialogue between Jesus and the Pharisees:

> Once Jesus was asked by the Pharisees when the kingdom of God was coming, and he answered, "The kingdom of God is not coming with things that can be observed; nor will they say, 'Look, here it is!' or 'There it is!' For, in fact, the kingdom of God is among you." (Luke 17:20–21)

Some translations render the last line, "the kingdom of God is *within you*." This leads some interpreters to give the saying a purely spiritual meaning, inferring that the kingdom was already present within the hearts of the Pharisees. This internalized meaning does not fit with the rest of Luke's Gospel and is very unlikely.

Jesus was pressed by the Pharisees for a prophecy of the precise time of the arrival of the kingdom. He rejected all speculation and calculation of the time or place of its coming. Rather, Jesus tried to turn the Pharisees' attention from the uncertain future to the concrete present: to the manifestations of God's reign already present in their midst, in the healing and teaching ministries of Jesus himself. "It is right here, it is what you see all around you."

Two additional texts, nearly identical, in the Gospels of Matthew and Luke, give added weight to the present, partial realization of the reign of God. Jesus spoke to his disciples of the blessing (or happiness or beatitude) that is theirs for being able to witness the wonders of God coming in power. They are sometimes called the privileges of discipleship.

> Then turning to the disciples Jesus said to them privately, "Blessed are the eyes that see what you see! For I tell you that many prophets and kings desired to see what you see, but did not see it, and to hear what you hear, but did not hear it." (Luke 10:23–24)

Jesus spoke to his followers of the privilege and beatitude that is theirs to be eyewitnesses of the wonders that they see and the teachings that they hear in the company of Jesus. Many of the great prophets and kings of Israel longed to see and hear the fulfillment of God's promise of salvation, these signs of the reign of God, but it was not yet time. The disciples were truly blessed to witness these wonders of salvation. In seeing and hearing what Jesus does and says, they experienced, at least partially, in their present, what the great figures of Israel's past could only hope for. The words *kingdom of God* are not specifically used, but the reality that the disciples are experiencing is the same. They are privileged to witness the coming of the kingdom in the ministry of Jesus.

One further text illustrates the present reality of the reign of God. It involves the issue of fasting. Jesus was asked why his disciples did not fast, while the disciples of John the Baptist and of the Pharisees did fast as a spiritual discipline.

> Now John's disciples and the Pharisees were fasting; and people came and said to him, "Why do John's disciples and the disciples of the Pharisees fast, but your disciples do not fast?" Jesus said to them, "The wedding-guests cannot fast while the bridegroom is with them, can they? As long as they have the bridegroom with them, they cannot fast. The days will come when the bridegroom is taken away from them, and then they will fast on that day." (Mark 2:18–20)

Jesus made present the scene of a wedding feast with the bridegroom and his bride in joyful celebration. In such a setting fasting, a gesture of sorrow or mourning, would be out of the question, unthinkable. Jesus depicts the marriage of the Messiah with the people of Israel as a joyful time of salvation. It is impossible for his disciples, his closest friends at the wedding, to fast while the bridegroom is still with them. But the day will come "when the bridegroom is taken away from them," referring to the violent death on the cross that will forcibly separate Jesus from his disciples. Then, indeed, it will be completely appropriate for his disciples to fast as a sign of their sorrow and mourning.

But at the present time, the bridegroom is still with them, teaching and performing wonders of healing. It is a time of joy and fellowship; it is the time of the inbreaking of the reign of God, visible in the ministry of Jesus. There can be no question of penitential fasting when God's saving actions are clearly visible in the work of Jesus.

In summary of this section we can conclude that several of the sayings and actions of Jesus argue strongly for the view that Jesus at times spoke of the kingdom as already present in some way in his ministry. Jesus's exorcisms are a particular illustration of this. In effect he declared his exorcisms to be both manifestations and at least partial realizations of God's coming in power to rule his people in the end time, and that time was imminent.

God's Reign as Coming in the Future

Jesus preached about the kingdom of God as a future yet imminent reality. It was an essential part of Jesus's message, in addition to and more prominent than his sayings about the reign of God already begun or partially being realized in his own time.

The most familiar and prominent of these sayings of Jesus is in the Our Father prayer, "Your kingdom come" (Matt 6:10; Luke 11:2). Jesus taught his disciples to pray in this way, addressing themselves to his Father, not as distant or remote, but as "my own dear Father" *(abba)*, familiar, personal, and endearing.

The first petition, "Hallowed be your name," asks God to sanctify his name by revealing his power and glory, by manifesting his saving authority for all of Israel as well as all of humankind to see. Only God can do this; Jesus's prayer is for the Father to show his powerful, creative, and saving self to our world.

The second petition, "Your kingdom come," is a close parallel to the first. Jesus is praying, "Come, O Father, to rule as king." Jesus was aware, from the Jewish tradition, that God was creator and exercised his kingly rule over the entire history of Israel. But Jesus also believed, as reflected in his prayerful petition for God to come and rule as king, that God, in some sense, was not yet fully ruling as king.

Jesus's petition refers to the future, to the definitive coming of God to reign as king. Jesus taught his disciples to pray for the longed-for coming of God as the king who would manifest his power and glory by regathering Israel in the end time. It is a statement of eschatological desire. Yet this almighty king of creation and history is addressed by Jesus's disciples as their own dear father.

In the only prayer that Jesus ever taught his disciples the first concern is not a need or problem of the present world but rather a strictly eschatological desire for God to reveal himself in all his power and glory by coming to Israel to reign fully and definitively as king. This coming of the eschatological kingdom of God was at the center of Jesus's message and hopes (Meier II, 298–302).

At the very end of his public life Jesus made a significant statement in the context of the last supper that relates to the kingdom of God. Just after he and his disciples drank from a cup of wine at the end of the meal, Jesus said, "Truly I tell you, I will never again drink of the fruit of the vine until that day when I drink it new in the kingdom of God" (Mark 14:25). At this solemn moment, and with an emphatic introduction, Jesus prophesied his death. He will not drink wine again at a festive meal until a future event occurs, namely, when he drinks it anew in the kingdom of God.

The setting for the scene at the last supper was that Jesus's ministry, from a human perspective, had been largely a failure. The people of Israel had not heeded his message and accepted him as the eschatological prophet sent by God. Moreover, he was aware that the possibility of a violent death loomed over him, that his death was probably near at hand.

But these words at the end of the meal were not a cry of desperation, because Jesus believed that God would vindicate his cause and his prophecy by bringing his kingdom and seating Jesus at the final banquet to drink the festive wine once again. This was a cry of hope from Jesus, expressing his trust in the God who will make his kingdom come despite Jesus's death. What is central in the thought and conviction of Jesus was not himself or his personal fate, but the final victory of God, who comes to rule his creation and his rebellious people, in other words, the kingdom of God. Jesus looked forward to the future coming of God's reign, and continued to do so even at the end of his life (Meier II, 306–9).

Another saying of Jesus about the kingdom of God is found in both the Gospels of Matthew and Luke, although in slightly different forms. The text as presented by Matthew is inserted into the miracle story of the healing of the centurion's servant. The centurion came to Jesus as he entered the town of Capernaum and asked him to cure the centurion's servant, who was at home, paralyzed, and in terrible distress. Jesus offered to come and cure him.

> The centurion answered, "Lord, I am not worthy to have you come under my roof; but only speak the word, and my servant will be healed. For I also am a man under authority, with soldiers under me." . . . When Jesus heard him, he was amazed and said to those who followed him, "Truly, I tell you, in no one in Israel have I found such faith. I tell

you many will come from east and west and will eat with
Abraham and Isaac and Jacob in the kingdom of heaven,
while the heirs of the kingdom will be thrown into the
outer darkness, where there will be weeping and gnashing
of teeth." And to the centurion Jesus said, "Go; let it be
done for you according to your faith." And the servant was
healed in that hour. (Matt 8:5–13)

In the process of praising the centurion's faith and contrasting it
with an unbelieving Israel, Jesus said that "the heirs of the kingdom" (Israel) will be rejected. This is a prophecy of judgment on
the last day. Multitudes will come from east and west and will
feast with the long-dead patriarchs of Israel at the same banquet.
The prophecy promises eschatological salvation in the kingdom
of God for some (Gentiles) and threatens definitive exclusion
from the kingdom for others (Jews who rejected Jesus). The passage indicates that the historical Jesus expected a future coming
of God's kingdom, a kingdom that transcended barriers of time,
space, hostility between Jews and Gentiles, and even death itself
(Meier II, 314–17).

Jesus's teaching in the beatitudes confirms his conviction
about the imminent coming of the kingdom of God. The beatitudes are found in two different forms: (1) in the Gospels of
Luke, where Jesus is pictured speaking to his disciples in a plain;
and (2) in the Gospel of Matthew, where Jesus is seen addressing his disciples as part of his sermon on the mount. The Lucan
version is succinct:

> Blessed are you who are poor, for yours is the
> kingdom of God.
> Blessed are you who are hungry now, for you
> shall be filled.
> Blessed are you who weep now, for you will
> laugh.
> Blessed are you when people hate you, and
> when they exclude you, revile you, and
> defame you on account of the Son of
> Man. Rejoice on that day and leap for joy,
> for surely your reward is great in heaven;

> for that is what their ancestors did to the
> prophets. (Luke 6:20–23, cf. Matt 5:3-11)

The contrast experiences Jesus described in the beatitudes re-flected his expectation that the kingdom of God was imminent. God is about to take charge over his rebellious creation and set things right. The poor are blessed because God is about to inaugurate his reign.

The background for the beatitudes is the Old Testament picture of God as the just king of the covenant community of Israel, the king who defends widows and orphans, secures the rights of the oppressed, and sees that justice is done. (For an explicit example of this vision, see Psalm 146:5–10.) It is this expectation that puts the promise of the kingdom of God first among the beatitudes. Jesus saw the definitive arrival of God's kingly rule as imminent.

> At the heart of Jesus's message is the promise of the defini-tive coming of God as king, who will bring to an end the present state of things by revealing himself in all his power and glory. In the kingdom that he will establish, he will vindicate those who unjustly suffer in this world: the sor-rowing will be comforted, the hungry will be fed to the full at the eschatological banquet [cf. the bread petition in the Lord's Prayer], the debt of sin will be remitted by God just as the saved will forgive one another's debt, and even the unclean Gentiles will be admitted to table fellowship with the patriarchs of Israel—as will Jesus himself, who will be saved out of death and brought into the kingdom he once proclaimed. In short, the core beatitudes cohere with and solidify the case for future eschatology . . . as an essential part of Jesus's preaching. (Meier II, 334)

If the historical Jesus of Nazareth was convinced that the definitive coming of God to rule over and save his people was imminent, it is fair to ask *how* imminent did he think it was. Was it coming "very soon," or was it in the indefinite future, at a time that was unpredictable?

There are three passages in the Gospels of Matthew and Mark that seem to indicate that Jesus thought God's rule was coming soon, within the lifetime of his contemporaries. At the end of Jesus's instructions to the chosen twelve of his disciples in preparation for their mission, he warned them of persecutions that lie ahead:

> You will be hated by all because of my name. But the one who endures to the end will be saved. When they persecute you in one town, flee to the next; for truly I tell you, you will not have gone through all the towns of Israel before the Son of Man comes. (Matt 10:22–23)

In another place Jesus spoke to the crowd and his disciples about what it meant to be his follower. "And he said to them, 'Truly I tell you, there are some standing here who will not taste death until they see that the kingdom of God has come with power'" (Mark 9:1).

Finally, near the end of his life, Jesus spoke to four of his disciples on the Mount of Olives opposite the temple area. He delivered an eschatological discourse, describing the persecutions and tribulations that will come before the Messiah will come in glory:

> Then they will see "the son of Man coming in clouds" (Dan 7:13) with great power and glory. . . . From the fig tree learn its lesson: as soon as its branch becomes tender and puts forth its leaves, you know that summer is near. So also, when you see these things taking place, you know that he is near, at the very gates. Truly I tell you, this generation will not pass away until all these things have taken place. Heaven and earth will pass away, but my words will not pass away. (Mark 13:26, 28–31)

All three of these texts give the impression that Jesus expected the definitive reign of God to come soon, if not right away, at least within the lifetimes of some of those presently living. But the exegetes insist that in all three of these instances, the words are not those of the historic Jesus of Nazareth. They are modifications inserted later by the evangelists, writing in the context of the early Christian churches, to account for the fact that the events predicted by Jesus had not yet come despite the passing of several decades after his death. Many of those who had expected to see the Lord's return had died. In all three cases words of assurance and consolation are given in the form of prophetic revelations of an eschatological future.

> The three sayings do not come from the historical Jesus. Most likely they were formulated by Christian prophets as words of consolation, encouragement, and direction to first-generation Christians who were facing both increasing hostility and an unexpectedly lengthy interval between resurrection and parousia. The upshot . . . is that, while Jesus proclaimed an imminent, definitive coming of God's kingdom, he did not specify any timetable or time limit for this coming.
>
> What we see in the case of these three sayings is not Christians inventing future eschatology out of whole cloth and imposing it on an uneschatological Jesus. Rather, faced with the given of Jesus' proclamation of an eschatological kingdom coming in the near future, the first generation Christians are producing sayings that seek to adjust Jesus's imminent eschatology to their own lived experience and resulting problems. . . . Imminent-future eschatology has its origins in Jesus; attempts to set time limits for that eschatology have their origin in the early church. (Meier II, 348)

Conclusion

Jesus's proclamation of the kingdom of God was central to his mission and ministry, not only in his sayings, but also in his actions. His exorcisms, other miraculous deeds of healing, his formation of an inner circle of twelve disciples, prefiguring the regathering of the twelve tribes of Israel, his table fellowship with tax collectors and sinners, his cleansing of the temple in Jerusalem—in all of these Jesus "acted out" his main message about the saving God coming to rule over his people and his creation.

> The kingdom of God that Jesus preached in word and action is not primarily a state or place but rather the entire dynamic event of God coming in power to rule his people

in the end time. It is a tensive symbol, a multi-faceted reality, a whole mythic story in miniature that cannot be grasped in a single formula or definition. This is why Jesus can speak of kingdom as both imminent and yet present. (Meier II, 452)

When Jesus said, "If it is by the finger of God that I cast out demons, then the kingdom of God has come to you" (Luke 11:20), he was declaring that his hearers were experiencing the kingdom already come. His powerful deeds are equated with the actions of God assuming his control of Israel in the end time, actions that are already happening and will soon be completed. His own actions are part of God's eschatological drama that is already under way and will soon be concluded. "God's liberating power in favor of his people Israel is already being experienced by those Israelites who have encountered it in Jesus" (Meier II, 453).

Chapter 4

The People of God, the Holy Spirit, and the Reign of God

It all comes together in the people of God. The two themes that we have been relentlessly pursuing—(1) the history of the Holy Spirit, in the scriptures and in the church's further reflections, and (2) the reign of God as proclaimed by Jesus of Nazareth—converge in the new people of God.

In philosophical terms the evolution of the people of God is guided and propelled by the Holy Spirit as its *efficient cause,* the force that moves it. Simultaneously, that evolution is pulled along, drawn forward, as its *final cause* by the reign of God, its ultimate goal.

In the words of the solemn teaching of the Second Vatican Council's *Dogmatic Constitution on the Church (LG):*

> The mystery of the holy church is clearly visible in its foundation. For the Lord Jesus inaugurated the church when he preached the happy news of the coming of the kingdom of God.... "The time is fulfilled and the kingdom of God is at hand" (Mark 1:15).
>
> Then when Christ, having undergone the death of the cross for humanity rose from the dead, he appeared as Lord and Christ . . . and poured on his disciples the Spirit that had been promised by the Father (Acts 2:33). When, therefore, the church, equipped with the gifts of its founder . . . receives the mission of announcing the kingdom of Christ and God and of inaugurating it among all peoples,

it has formed the seed and the beginning of the kingdom on earth. Meanwhile . . . it aspires after the completion of the kingdom, and hopes and desires with all its strength to be joined with its king in glory. (*LG*, no. 5)

This [messianic] people has been given the dignity and the freedom of the sons and daughters of God, in whose hearts the holy Spirit dwells as in a temple. For its law it has the new commandment of love just as Christ has loved us (see John 13:34). And finally it has as its goal the kingdom of God, inaugurated on earth by God himself and to be further extended until, at the end of time, it will be brought to its completion by the Lord when Christ will appear, our life (see Col 3:4), and "creation itself will be set free from its bondage to decay and obtain the glorious liberty of the children of God" (Rom 8:21). (*LG*, no. 9)

All the elements of the converging evolution of the people of God, epitomized by the church (but not equated with the church) are here: Jesus's proclamation of the kingdom, already present on earth and awaited at the end time, the church's mission to announce and promote the kingdom, the gift of the Holy Spirit, the powerful yearning for the coming reign of God, and the recognition that it will affect all of creation.

The People of God

God chose the people of Israel as a people for himself; he made a covenant with them; and he instructed them, making his intentions known to them and sanctifying them for himself. "I will be your God and you shall be my people" (Lev 26:12).

For you are a people holy to the Lord, your God; he has chosen you out of all the peoples on earth to be his people, his treasured possession. It was not because you were more numerous than any other people that the Lord set his heart on you and chose you . . . It was because the Lord loved you and kept the oath that he swore to your ancestors, that the Lord has brought you out with a mighty hand, and redeemed you from the house of slavery. (Deut 7:6–8)

The chosen people did not always keep their part of the covenant with God, and the prophets spoke of the need for a new covenant:

> The days are surely coming, says the Lord, when I will make a new covenant with the house of Israel and the house of Judah. It will not be like the covenant that I made with their ancestors when I took them by hand to bring them out of the land of Egypt—a covenant that they broke. . . . But this is the covenant that I will make with the house of Israel after those days, says the Lord: I will put my law within them, and I will write it on their hearts; and I will be their God and they shall be my people. (Jer 31:31–33)

A New Covenant

It is to this new covenant that Jesus referred at his last supper with his disciples when he said, "This cup that is poured out for you is the new covenant in my blood" (Luke 22:20). It is a covenant that called together both Jews and Gentiles, bound together in unity by the Holy Spirit, to be the new people of God. The apostle Peter, or someone in his tradition, writing to early Christian churches in Asia Minor, described them as "a chosen race, a royal priesthood, a holy nation, God's own people . . . once no people but now God's people" (1 Pet 2:9–10).

This establishment of the new people of God in Christ does not imply a repudiation of Jews or an annulment of the Mosaic covenant with the tribes of Israel. God's choice of the Jewish people continues: "I ask, then, has God rejected his people? By no means! . . . God has not rejected his people whom he foreknew" (Rom 11:1–2).

The new people of God in Christ encompasses all the world's Christians, all of those who believe in Jesus of Nazareth as the author of salvation. It includes all communities of Jesus's disciples—Catholic, Protestant, Orthodox, Pentecostal, and others. "All human beings are called to the new people of God. . . . For all the nations of the earth, therefore, there is one people of God,

since it draws its citizens from all nations" (*LG,* no. 13). All look
to Jesus in faith as the principle of unity and peace.

> Therefore, to this catholic unity of the people of God,
> which prefigures and promotes universal peace, all are
> called, and they belong to it or are ordered to it in various
> ways, whether they be catholic faithful or others who be-
> lieve in Christ, or finally all people everywhere who by the
> grace of God are called to salvation. (*LG,* no. 13)

Catholic Church

The Catholic Church, like the other Christian churches, is one
portion or segment of the new people of God. The "catholic
faithful" are defined as those who are incorporated into Christ
through baptism and thus constituted as the people of God and
are deemed "fully incorporated" into the church in the following way:

> They are fully incorporated into the society of the church
> who, possessing the Spirit of Christ, accept its whole
> structure and all the means of salvation that have been
> established within it, and within its visible framework are
> united with Christ, who governs it through the supreme
> pontiff and the bishops, by the bonds of profession of faith,
> the sacraments, ecclesiastical government and communion.
> (*LG,* no. 14)

These elements of full incorporation quite clearly identify those
who are full members of the Catholic Church, a significant portion of the entire people of God in Christ.

People of God and Reign of God

The Catholic Church, and even the entire worldwide people of
God, is *not* the kingdom of God. The two are not to be confused
or conflated. This has been misunderstood at times in the past.
Some have identified the church on earth with the reign of God.

The two realities are quite distinct, but not unrelated. What is the relationship between the church and the kingdom?

The people of God, and the church as one embodiment of that people, is a *sacrament* of the reign of God. The community of Christ's faithful people is the visible sign of the invisible reality of the kingdom. The people of God, and the church within it, points to the reign of God insofar as it is still hidden and incomplete.

The people of God is not the reign of God, nor can it create God's rule; the reign of God is the work of God, not the work of humankind. It is not like a skyscraper, a high rise built up by workers from below. The reign of God was proclaimed and initiated by Jesus of Nazareth in the first century—his miracles signaled the first inbreaking of that reign. The new people of God, brought together by the risen Christ and the Holy Spirit, assume the mission of announcing and fostering that reign.

The new people of God unceasingly proclaims the coming reign of God. It does so by constant preaching of the gospel, in teaching, and in prayer. Billions of times each day Christians pray "your kingdom come" in the Lord's prayer. At eucharistic celebrations the world over they are asked to drink from the chalice of Christ's blood, "the blood of the new and eternal covenant." They proclaim his death and profess his resurrection "until you come again" after the consecration. They pray for their departed brothers and sisters that they be admitted to God's kingdom, "where we hope to enjoy forever the fullness of your glory." In these prayers and countless other ways the people of God reminds its members and announces to the world the reign of God yet to come.

In addition to this constant proclamation, the churches' actions and projects serve as "already" instances of God's reign, models of what lies ahead, the "not yet" in the fulfillment of that reign. Schools of all kinds and levels serve to develop the human potential and level of culture. Hospitals, clinics, and healthcare initiatives, reflective of Jesus's own healings and exorcisms, relieve pain and extend life. Charitable institutions, soup kitchens, and clothes closets attempt to alleviate the burdens of the poor. The sacraments of baptism, penance, and Eucharist offer forgiveness and reconciliation. Agencies for conflict resolution and peacemaking help to prevent violence and promote justice. These and many other programs and projects are the visible signs that churches are sacraments of the coming reign of God.

The Final Age

This concept of the people of God connects to the historical precedents of God's covenant with the people of Israel and to the present situation of the whole church moving forward, evolving, on its eschatological pilgrimage toward its final fulfillment. The people of God live in the "between" times, between the Christ event—the coming of Jesus, his public ministry, his death and resurrection, and the outpouring of the Spirit—and the second coming of Christ—the arrival of God's reign, the fulfillment of humankind and of the universe itself, a new creation.

The final age of the world has come upon the people of God through the work of the risen Christ and his life-giving Spirit. Christ and his Spirit are at work in human hearts instilling a desire for the world to come and at the same time animating the aspirations of the human family to make its present life more human. They prompt the members of God's people to devote themselves to the service of humanity and in this way prepare for God's future reign.

Our expectation of a new earth should stimulate our resolve to cultivate our present earth in ways that even now can foreshadow the new age. *Gaudium et spes (Pastoral Constitution on the Church in the Modern World)* puts it this way: "Although earthly progress must be carefully distinguished from the growth of God's kingdom, nevertheless its capacity to contribute to a better ordering of human society makes it highly relevant to the kingdom of God" (*GS*, no. 39). A better ordering of human society, with values of human dignity, fellowship, and freedom, one which brings closer real justice and true peace, disposes our world to that time when

> Christ hands over to the Father an eternal and universal kingdom: "a kingdom of truth and life, of holiness and grace, a kingdom of justice, love and peace." Here on earth that kingdom is already mysteriously present; at the Lord's coming it will be consummated. (*GS*, no. 39)

All of the good works of the people of God, inspired by the Holy Spirit, prepare the way for the reign of God. God is personally present and active in all of these initiatives, just as he was in creation and the incarnation.

The Holy Spirit and the Church

We have studied the self-revelation of the Holy Spirit in the scriptures and the church's centuries-long efforts to understand and describe the reality of the Spirit. Now it is time to reflect on the ways in which the Spirit affects the church, one of the portions of the entire people of God.

The Second Vatican Council that took place in Rome between 1962 and 1965 has been viewed as a major step forward in our understanding of and appreciation for the Holy Spirit. It was a major event in the Catholic pneumatological (the theology of the Spirit) renaissance. We draw upon the relevant teachings of the council as well as the foregoing reflections in an attempt to outline the areas of influence of the Spirit on the life of the church.

The Holy Spirit Animates the Church

The Spirit gives life, unity, and movement to the whole body of Christ, which is the church, and for that reason is compared to the life principle, the soul in the human body. Augustine of Hippo wrote, "The holy spirit acts in the entire church, as does the soul in all the members of the human body" (see *LG*, no. 7; *Ad gentes [AG]*, no. 4).

> It is . . . by no mean analogy that it [the church] is likened to the mystery of the Word incarnate. For just as the assumed nature serves the divine Word as a living instrument of salvation, . . . in a similar way the social structure of the church serves the Spirit of Christ who vivifies the church toward the growth of the body (see Eph 4:16). (*LG*, no. 8)

The Holy Spirit functions like the soul of the church and, as such, is the vital source of all of the church's activities.

The Holy Spirit Is the Principle of the Church's Communion

The Spirit is the source and seal of the church's unity and cohesion that is called communion (*communio* in Latin, *koinonia* in Greek). *Communion* names the graced connection of the baptized to the Triune God and to one another. It is the profound and mysterious bond of unity that is manifested in common faith, sacraments, authority, and even financial aid. It is the Holy Spirit that unites the church in fellowship *(communio)* and in ministry (*LG*, no. 4).

> For this finally God sent the Spirit of his Son, the Lord and giver of life, who is for the whole church and for each and every one of the faithful the principle of union and unity in the teaching of the apostles, in communion, in the breaking of the bread and in prayers (see Acts 2:42). . . . For all the faithful scattered throughout the world are in communion with the rest in the Holy Spirit. (*LG*, no. 13)

Communion consists of living and behaving as a conscious member of an organic whole that is the church, and it is the work of the Holy Spirit.

The Holy Spirit Sanctifies the Church and Its Members

> When the task that the Father had entrusted to the Son on earth had been completed (see John 17:4), on the day of Pentecost the Holy Spirit was sent to sanctify the church continually and so that believers would have through Christ access to the Father in one Spirit (see Eph 2:18). . . . The Spirit dwells in the church and the hearts of the faithful as in a temple (see 1 Cor 3:16; 6:19). (*LG*, no. 4)

The Holy Spirit not only lives within the church as in a holy temple but gives grace to the church and its members; all of God's grace is given by the Spirit.

All of the church's worship is carried out in the Holy Spirit, to the Father, through the Son, in the Spirit. In the sacraments of Christian initiation catechumens receive the Spirit who makes them adopted children of God.

The Holy Spirit sanctifies the eucharistic offering each time it is celebrated. The congregation of the faithful, in the words of the presider, invokes the Spirit and recognizes that the gifts are sanctified through the Spirit's power. "Let your Spirit come upon these gifts to make them holy, so that they become for us the body and blood of our Lord Jesus Christ" (Eucharistic Prayer II).

Sin remains a reality in the church. The process of sanctification is an ongoing struggle, both in the communities of the pilgrim church and in its individual members. The church's need for conversion, repentance, purification, and renewal is constant (*LG*, nos. 8, 15).

The Holy Spirit brings forgiveness of sins. After his resurrection Jesus said to his disciples, "'As the Father has sent me, so I send you.' And when he had said this, he breathed on them and said to them, 'Receive the Holy Spirit. If you forgive the sins of any, they are forgiven them; if you retain the sins of any, they are retained'" (John 20:22–23).

The Holy Spirit Preserves the Church in Truth

Dei verbum (Dogmatic Constitution on Divine Revelation) states: "The holy Spirit . . . is active, making the living voice of the gospel ring out in the church, and through it in the world, leading those who believe into the whole truth, and making the message of Christ dwell in them in all its richness" (*DV*, no. 8). The same Spirit that guided the writing of scripture is the Spirit of truth that enlightens the successors of the apostles in faithfully preserving, interpreting, and expounding the word of God (*DV*, no. 9).

The indwelling Spirit "leads the church into all truth (see John 16:13)" (*LG*, no. 4). The Holy Spirit, who receives the fullness of truth from the Father and the Son, communicates it to the church which that same Spirit guards from ever falling into error and assists in making God's teaching fruitful for people.

The Spirit arouses and sustains a supernatural sense of the faith in the universal body of the faithful, so that they cannot be mistaken in belief (*LG*, no. 12). The Spirit of truth helps believers to understand the correct meaning of the content of Christ's message.

The Holy Spirit Leads and Guides the Church

The community of the disciples of Christ is directed by the Holy Spirit in its pilgrimage toward the Father's kingdom (*GS*, no. 1). Just as the Spirit of the Lord came upon Christ and anointed him to preach the good news to the poor, so the Spirit, sent by Christ from the Father, directs the church as it attempts to bring Christ's message of salvation to all humankind. The Holy Spirit carries out Christ's saving work from within and moves the church toward its destined expansion. Indeed, the Holy Spirit is the principal agent of the whole of the church's mission.

On the day of Pentecost the Spirit descended on the disciples so as to remain with them forever, the church was made manifest, and the preaching of the gospel among the nations had its origin.

> For it was from Pentecost that the "acts of the apostles" began, just as Christ had been conceived by the descent of the Holy Spirit on the virgin Mary, and had been impelled to the task of his ministry by the same Holy Spirit who came upon him as he prayed. The same Lord Jesus . . . arranged the ministry of the apostles and promised the sending of the Holy Spirit, in such as way that both were to be associated always and everywhere in achieving the work of salvation. (*AG*, no. 4)

The Holy Spirit at times visibly initiated apostolic activity, for instance, when the Spirit fell upon Peter's listeners in the house of Cornelius, prompting the first baptism of Gentiles (Acts 10:44–47). And the Spirit accompanied and directed such activities in various ways, for example, when Peter spoke to the Sanhedrin (Acts 4:8), when Phillip encountered the Ethiopian (Acts 8:29ff.), when the prophet Agabus predicted a famine (Acts 11:27ff.), when Barnabas and Saul were selected and sent on mission (Acts 13:2ff.), when Paul and Timothy were prevented from preaching in the province of Asia and Bithynia (Acts 16:6–7), and when Paul was compelled by the Spirit to go to Jerusalem (Acts

20:22). In each of these events the intervention of the Spirit is explicitly mentioned.

The Holy Spirit Builds Up the Church by Means of Gifts

The Spirit apportions gifts to each person individually as the Spirit wills, and among the faithful of every rank the Spirit distributes special graces by which they are rendered fit and ready to undertake the various tasks and offices which help the renewal and building up of the church according to that word: "To each is given the manifestation of the Spirit for the common good" (1 Cor 12:7). "These charismatic gifts, whether they be very outstanding or simpler and more widely diffused, are to be accepted with thanksgiving and consolation, since they are primarily suited to and useful for the needs of the Church" (*LG*, no. 12). The Holy Spirit is the source of these charismatic gifts, both ordinary and exceptional.

The Holy Spirit gives special gifts to the faithful so that "as all use whatever gifts they have received in service to one another," they may be "good stewards dispensing the grace (*gratia*) of God in its varied forms" (1 Pet 4:10), toward the building up of the whole body in love (Eph 4:16). The Second Vatican Council's *Apostolicam actuositatem (Decree on the Apostolate of the Laity)* states:

> Through receiving these gifts of grace, however unspectacular, every one of the faithful has the right and duty to exercise them in the church and in the world for the good of humanity and for the building up of the church. They do this in the freedom of the Spirit who "blows where he wills" (John 3:8) and, at the same time, in communion with the fellowship in Christ, especially with his pastors, whose part it is to judge about their true nature and ordered use, not indeed so as to extinguish the Spirit but in order to test everything and to hold on to what is good (see 1 Thess 5:12, 19, 21). (*AA*, no. 3)

This charismatic element belongs to the very nature and life of the church. The gifts of the Spirit are not only present in the church, but they are *constitutive* of the church and its life. The charismatic factor is not just one part of the church's system, one that stands over against the institutional or hierarchical part, for charisms are given to officeholders as well as to others. Both hierarchical and charismatic gifts have their source in the same Spirit (*LG,* no. 4). Rather, the charismatic factor is a characteristic of the church's entire system as a whole, an openness to the One who is beyond it.

The Holy Spirit Renews the Church

The Spirit rejuvenates the church and continually renews it (*LG,* no. 4). As it journeys through the temptations and tribulations of this present world, the church "under the action of the Holy Spirit" does not cease from renewing itself (*LG,* no. 9). "Guided by the Holy Spirit" the church continually exhorts its children to purification and renewal so that the sign of Christ may shine more clearly on its face (*GS,* no. 43). In order to make God present to those around it, the church must continually renew and cleanse itself "under the guidance of the Holy Spirit" (*GS,* no. 21).

The Holy Spirit Is God's Pledge for the Future

The church journeys on its pilgrim path through history under the guidance of the Spirit, looking forward as well as backward. Christ, when lifted up from the earth, sent his life-giving Spirit down on his disciples, and through the Spirit he constituted the church as a sacrament of salvation. Its earthly project is advanced through the mission of the Holy Spirit and continues by means of the Spirit. The pilgrim church with its sacraments and institutions belongs to this age; it carries the figure of this world, which is passing. The end of the ages has reached us. Even so, the church is sealed by the Holy Spirit, "who is the first installment of our inheritance toward redemption" (Eph 1:14), and possesses the first fruits of the Spirit as it endures in hope (*LG,* no. 48). The Spirit comes to the aid of our weakness, and since we do not know how to pray as we ought, the Spirit intercedes for us with inexpressible groanings (Rom 8:23–26).

The Spirit is the earnest (the down payment, pledge, security) of things to come, the "promised One" (Luke 24:49; Acts 1:4; 2:33). The Spirit points to the future and constantly reminds the church that everything is provisional as we await the fulfillment of all things in Christ.

Summary

These several affirmations of the Holy Spirit's influences over the church assert the various kinds of sway of the Spirit over the life and direction of the church. These statements are solemn and firm convictions derived from the most recent ecumenical council, not mere theological speculations. They are matters of belief, that is, there are no scientific proofs of the Spirit's interventions in events in the life of the church. We believe that the Holy Spirit exercises its powers over the life of the people of God in these ways and that the Spirit is the animating force in the evolution of the church.

A question arises: If the Holy Spirit has these kinds of assistance and influence over the church, why isn't the church perfect? How can the church make mistakes, serious mistakes, sometimes catastrophic mistakes, as it makes its way through history? Think of events like the toleration of slavery, the Crusades, the excesses of the Inquisition, the denial of freedom of religion, or, in our own time, the clergy sex abuse of minors. If the Holy Spirit is guiding the church, how can such terrible things happen?

The answer lies in the humanity of the church and in the mode of the Spirit's interventions. The church, like each one of its members, is human, with the freedom to make mistakes, to do stupid things, to get it wrong, to be captivated by the surrounding culture, to capitulate to political pressures. And the way that the Spirit guides the church, as well as its individual members, is not by force, compulsion, or other infringements on human freedom. It isn't like a steersman directing a ship or a driver controlling an automobile. The Spirit communicates in subtle ways, in the voices of prophets, in persons of insight, in the discernment of groups of believers, in response to prayer. Sometimes these voices are heard and heeded; sometimes they are repressed or ignored. But they must always be sought out, searched for, and listened to.

The Church and the Reign of God

The church is one portion of the new people of God. It lives in history, in the time between the resurrection of Christ and his return, under the guidance of the Spirit, who is a pledge or down payment on its full inheritance, the reign of God. Stated simply, "it has as its goal the kingdom of God" (*LG,* no. 9)

Jesus of Nazareth proclaimed and preached and actually began the reign of God while he lived on this earth. After Jesus's departure from earth the church took on his mission and ministry regarding God's reign. It is not only the message of the church, but it is its objective, the goal toward which it constantly strives.

We attempted (in Chapter 3) to describe what Jesus meant by the reign of God. It was not a place, a territory, here on earth or off in heaven, but the whole process of God coming in power to establish his definitive rule in Israel and the world. Jesus, in his ministry, focused on the peoples and lands of Israel, but his message far transcended those tribes and territories. Let us briefly recall that description.

The reign of God stands for the whole *story* of God's saving actions, for God's powerful rule as king over his people and his creation. It tells of God's actions upon and his relationships with those over whom he rules. It is a dynamic, ongoing, *happening* involving God and God's people, and eventually all of creation.

Jesus did not paint a picture of what the reign of God will look like, nor did he leave a detailed description of it, but, if it is to be the church's goal and striving, it is necessary to find some sense of its content, its substance, a more vivid description of its meaning. Jesus did leave some markers, some directions in which to look to find its meaning more concretely.

Jesus's Wonderworks

Jesus's own actions in his ministry marked the inbreaking of the reign of God. For example, Jesus told the disciples of John the Baptist:

> "Go and tell John what you hear and see: the blind receive their sight, the lame walk, the lepers are cleansed, the deaf

hear, the dead are raised, and the poor have the good news brought to them. And blessed is anyone who takes no offense at me." (Matt 11:2–6)

We can extrapolate from those beginnings to what the "further extension" of the reign should be: the blind receive sight, the lame walk, lepers are cleansed, the deaf hear, the dead are raised, and the poor hear good news. Not all of these are miraculous, and the church is and should be engaged in relieving many of these human needs by its healing and caring resources. These are some of the strivings toward the reign of God. They include local efforts, such as the St. Vincent de Paul Society's direct assistance to the poor in parishes, and such sweeping national and international initiatives as Catholic Relief Services and the Campaign for Human Development.

Exorcisms

Jesus's exorcisms provide another example. He relieved the sufferings of deeply disturbed people, liberating them from the compulsions that bound them and deprived them of their freedom. Such tangible interventions not only freed the sick persons but affected their families and neighbors. These transforming gestures of returning the mentally troubled to health are another indicator of the "look" of God's reign that is made real in the work of psychiatrists, doctors, nurses, and the thousands of others who care for the mentally ill today.

Gathering

Jesus raised another "signal" of the coming reign of God when he spoke of the gathering of the tribes of Israel and named the twelve who represented those ancient tribes. The gathering of the scattered people of God was a basic theme of Israel's theological history:

When all these things have happened to you, the blessings and curses that I have set before you, if you call them to mind among all the nations where the Lord your God has driven you, and return to the Lord your God, and you and your children obey him with all your heart and all your soul, just as I am commanding you today, then the Lord your God will restore your fortunes and have compassion on you, gathering you from all the peoples among whom the Lord your God has scattered you. Even if you are exiled to the ends of the world, from there the Lord your God will gather you, and from there he will bring you back. (Deut 30:1–4)

This gathering of Israel from the diaspora represented the salvation of the people, tantamount to their liberation or redemption. It was the work of God and symbolized the way that God acts toward his people. It was repeated by the prophets and in the everyday prayers of the people.

Jesus knew of this theme and made it his own: "Whoever is not with me is against me, and whoever does not gather with me scatters" (Matt 12:30). And "Jerusalem, Jerusalem. . . . How often have I desired to gather your children together as a hen gathers her brood under her wings and you were not willing!" (Matt 23:37). Jerusalem stands for all Israel.

Hallowed Be Your Name

The first petition in prayer that Jesus taught his disciples, the Our Father, is "hallowed be your name." This touchstone phrase summarizes the familiar theme of the profaning and sanctifying of God's name linked with the dispersal and gathering of the people. It is spelled out by the prophet Ezekiel:

I scattered [the Israelites] among the nations, and they were dispersed through the countries; in accordance with their conduct and their deeds I judged them. But when they came to the nations, wherever they came, they profaned my holy name, in that it was said of them, "These are the people of the Lord, and yet they had to go out of his land." But I had concern for my holy name, which the house of Israel had profaned among the nations to which they came.

Therefore say to the house of Israel, Thus says the Lord God: It is not for your sake, O house of Israel, that I am about to act, but for the sake of my holy name, which you

have profaned among the nations to which you came. I will
sanctify my great name which has been profaned among
the nations, and which you have profaned among them;
and the nations shall know that I am the Lord, says the
Lord God, when through you I display my holiness before
their eyes. I will take you from the nations and gather you
from all the countries, and bring you into your own land.
. . . A new heart I will give you, and a new spirit I will put
within you; and I will remove from your body the heart
of stone and give you a heart of flesh. I will put my spirit
within you, and make you follow my statutes and be careful to obey my ordinances. Then you shall live in the land
that I gave to your ancestors, and you shall be my people,
and I will be your God. (Ezek 36:19–28)

"Hallowed be your name." Jesus called up this whole drama
of alienation and restoration between Israel and its God and
epitomized it in one simple sentence, the first petition of the
Lord's prayer. It is a plea for the eschatological gathering and
restoration of the people of God.

The Twelve

In addition to prayer, Jesus took action. He chose twelve of his
disciples—chose them by name—and sent them out to proclaim
the reign of God throughout the land (Mark 3:13–19). It was the
beginning of the hoped-for restoration of the twelve tribes, described in Ezekiel 47—48. Jesus's creation of the twelve apostles
was a very deliberate sign of eschatological fulfillment. It was a
sign of the imminent coming of the reign of God.

Beatitudes

The series of blessings that Jesus called out in his sermon on the
plain, which are commonly known as the beatitudes, offers some
further directions for our search for the shape and content of the
coming reign of God.

> Blessed are you who are poor, for yours is the
> kingdom of God.

> Blessed are you who are hungry now, for you
>   shall be filled.
> Blessed are you who weep now, for you will
>   laugh.
> Blessed are you when people hate you, and
>   when they exclude you, revile you, and
>   defame you on account of the Son of
>   Man. Rejoice on that day and leap for joy,
>   for surely your reward is great in heaven;
>   for that is what their ancestors did to the
>   prophets. (Luke 6:20–23; Matt 5:3–11)

For Jesus, these benefits for the needy and marginalized were about to arrive; they were on the way to the poor of Israel. We view them as promises yet to be fulfilled, but they give us ideas about the values of the end time and what the way toward that final fulfillment should look like.

They speak of the poor being cared for, of the hungry being fed (and fed well), the sorrowing being consoled (to the point of joy), and of the excluded and denounced being justified (and joyful). These projections about the coming reign of God provide some guidance for the church, one portion of the people of God, which awaits its arrival.

One of the Old Testament roots for the beatitudes gave a slightly different scope of issues characteristic of the reign of God:

> The LORD sets the prisoners free;
>   the LORD opens the eyes of the blind.
> The LORD lifts up those who are bowed down;
>   the LORD loves the righteous.
> The LORD watches over the strangers;
>   he upholds the orphan and the widow,
>   but the way of the wicked he brings to ruin.
> The LORD will reign forever,
>   your God, O Zion, for all generations.
> Praise the LORD! (Ps 146:5–10)

Jesus knew and prayed the psalms, and surely he patterned the beatitudes on this psalm. It depicts the Lord as a benign and benevolent king who cares for his people lovingly. Blessed are those who bring justice to the oppressed (by being held in bondage or by an occupying power); who feed the hungry; who free those imprisoned; who give sight to the blind (an idiom for freeing captives); who relieve the overburdened; who care for strangers, orphans, and widows who have no one to protect and support them. The whole range of what we call social concerns were envisioned as the concerns of the coming king.

Church

The church *is not* the reign of God, nor can the church create or even hasten the reign of God. The reign of God—the dynamic event of God coming in power to rule his people in the end time—is the work of God, not humankind. But that work is under way; it has begun; it is ongoing here and now, at present. The church, as sacrament of that reign, can read the foregoing signs and directions laid down by Jesus of Nazareth and work toward them. The church, as it strives toward the reign of God as its goal, can remove obstructions (or at least try to), enable things to happen, encourage and pursue the values and projects that Jesus has pointed out.

The church, as a part of the people of God, will continue to worship God, to teach and proclaim to the world the whole of salvation history, with the Christ event and the sending of the Spirit at its center. In word and sacrament it will embrace the reign of God as it approaches. The church, following the kingdom signs that Jesus bestowed on us, will evolve in the direction of the reign of God.

Chapter 5

Structural Developments in the Church's Evolution

Synodality

Pope Francis addressed the Synod of Bishops on October 17, 2015, the fiftieth anniversary of the founding of the synod by Pope Paul VI. Pope Paul envisioned the synod as a consultative body of bishops to share in the pope's solicitude for the universal church. The synod was to reproduce on a smaller scale the image of the Second Vatican Council and reflect its spirit and method. Pope Francis, in his talk given after fifty years of very mixed experiences of the synod, outlined a plan for making the synodal model a pattern for the renewal of the church today.

Pope Francis said that it is precisely this path of *synodality* that God expects of the church of the third millennium. He defined the word *synod* as "journeying together"—laity, pastors, and pope, all sharing in the journey. The whole body of the faithful has an anointing from the Holy Spirit. The Spirit dwells within each of the baptized as in a temple. The pope said that a synodal church is one that listens, one that realizes that listening is more than simply hearing—it is a mutual listening in which everyone has something to learn—the faithful people, their pastors, the bishops, and the bishop of Rome—all listening to one another and to the Holy Spirit, the Spirit of truth (John 14:17).

The concept of a synod stems from the experience of an assembly in the early church in Jerusalem to resolve the question of the admission of Gentiles alongside Jews as followers of Christ.

The dramatic event, often referred to as the Council of Jerusalem, is described at length in Acts 15. After much discussion and prayer the final decision was communicated with these words: "For it has seemed good to the Holy Spirit and to us to impose on you no further burden than these essentials" (Acts 15:28). The apostles and elders were conscious that the Spirit was with them in their discernment.

Ever since that time a conciliar or synodal (the terms are almost interchangeable) process has been the church's favored way of clarifying teachings, making changes in structures, and modifying policies. Francis has said that synodality is a constitutive element of the church.

The pope went on to outline how this synodal pattern finds expression at the different levels of the church, and how its exercise is manifested in different ways in the canon law of the church. What follows are the structures mentioned by the pope, plus a few more.

Parish

The first expression of synodality is at the level of the local congregation—the parish or other local faith community. This is where the church is most real, where people know and care about one another, where the gospel is preached, where the mystery of the Lord's supper is celebrated, where adults teach children about Jesus. Synodality exists at this level in the parish council, the finance council, the various committees and organizations, that, under the guidance of the pastor and other ministers, make the parish live. Vatican II's *Lumen gentium (Dogmatic Constitution on the Church)* states: "In their own locality these are the new people called by God in the Holy Spirit. . . . In these communities . . . Christ is present by whose power the one, holy catholic and apostolic church is gathered together" (*LG*, no. 26).

Diocese

At the level of the diocesan church, synodality is exercised by the diocesan synod, wherein laity, priests, and religious come together with the bishop for the benefit of the whole community. But such diocesan synods are held rarely, and with mixed results.

Some do succeed in energizing the diocese and giving new direction to its ministries. Other "organs of communion" (as Pope Francis called them) in the diocesan church are the presbyteral council, the college of consultors, and the pastoral council. The last of these, the diocesan pastoral council, another hopeful innovation from the Second Vatican Council, comprises mostly lay people, with some clergy and religious, led by the bishop or his delegate. Its purpose is to investigate, consider, and propose practical conclusions regarding pastoral works in the diocese. A suspicion persists that diocesan pastoral councils have not been very successful as planning or policymaking bodies, but instead serve only as venues for listening and sharing. To the extent that these structures remain connected to the people of God, with their daily problems, needs, and viewpoints, a synodal church can begin to take shape. Even when these means prove wearisome, Pope Francis said, they must be taken seriously and valued as opportunities for listening and sharing.

Province

This is the much-neglected middle level of church structures between the diocese and the national church. This level, once occupied by influential archbishops and their regional bishops, has been eroded from above by the Roman Curia's tendency toward centralized control, and from below by the reluctance of local bishops to limit their autonomy. Ecclesiastical provinces led by their metropolitans exist, but as organizational structures they are weak and largely ineffectual. Provincial councils are provided for in canon law to respond to the pastoral needs of the people of God in the ecclesiastical province, and, in addition to the bishops of the province, many others, men and women, religious and lay, may be invited to take part, but with only a consultative vote. Such councils have legislative power, and while they have been historically significant, they are never held now. Should this tradition be rethought and revived?

Nation

At the national level, the United States Conference of Catholic Bishops does exist and is very active. It coordinates and promotes many ministries and the national mission of the church; it also lobbies government agencies on behalf of Catholic causes. However, it is composed of bishops only, not a council that includes other ministers and members of the church. For that reason the conference is not an ideal synodal structure. It enjoys some lawmaking power, but the scope of its authority is limited by the restrictions imposed by canon law and the legitimate authority of diocesan bishops. The conference has a National Advisory Council made up of lay people, deacons, religious, and priests, which gives some voice to the larger church at the national level.

Canon law also provides for a plenary council for the whole country (or the region of the conference of bishops), with wide representative membership and broad legislative authority. The three plenary councils of Baltimore held in the nineteenth century were very influential in the formation of American Catholicism. Today, plenary councils are never held (but one was seriously proposed in the early 2000s to deal with the clergy sexual-abuse scandal).

Supra-national

In addition to the foregoing canonical structures, there are several supra-national or continental gatherings of bishops such as the Council of Bishops of Latin America (CELAM), the Council of Episcopal Conferences of Europe (CCEE), and the Federation of Asian Bishops' Conferences (FABC). These councils promote cooperation and coordination of pastoral efforts across national boundaries, but they have little authority and mostly involve communications among bishops' conferences within their geographical regions.

Beside the full, international assemblies of the Synod of Bishops, referred to below, several regional or continental "special" synods have been held for Africa, America, Asia, Oceania, and Europe. These have been one-time events.

Universal

The last level of synodality, that of the church universal, finds expression in the international Synod of Bishops, made up of a representative group of bishops (between 150 and 250 in number) mostly elected by their national conferences. It convenes in Rome every two to four years for a period of three or four weeks. It is a very modest expression of collegiality within a church that aspires to be truly synodal, joining the bishops among themselves in consultation with the pope. Its role (so far) is purely consultative, not determinative. Francis has tried to enhance the Synod of Bishops, which he considers a precious legacy of the Second Vatican Council.

The challenge at every level of synodality is active participation, dynamic leadership, and effectiveness. Most synodal bodies are organs of *consultation* within the various levels of ecclesial communion. For the most part, they are not legislative. However, they can be effective instruments of participation, listening, learning, and even policy formation.

Newer means of communication can facilitate these synodal instruments of communion—simultaneous translation, conference calls, television, Skype, and email are some examples—when logistical problems or large geographical distances make regular meetings difficult.

Innovations or developments along "this path of *synodality* which God expects of the church of the third millennium," in the words of Pope Francis, should be viewed through the lens of the principle of subsidiary function, and not merely as matters of decentralization. Decentralization is needed, especially with regard to the Roman Curia in relationship to bishops' conferences, ecclesiastical provinces, and individual dioceses, but decentralization speaks of breaking down bureaucracies, distribution of tasks, and efficiency of administration.

According to John Paul II's encyclical letter *Centesimus annus,* the principle of subsidiary function means that "a community of a higher order should not interfere in the internal life of a community of a lower order, depriving the latter of its functions, but rather should support it in a case of need, and help to coordinate its activities with the rest of society, always with a view to the common good" (*CA,* no. 48). It is a longstanding principle of Catholic social teaching that has been explicitly applied within the church by Pope Pius XII and Pope Paul VI and was included in the principles to guide the revision of the Code of Canon Law in 1969. It stands for the legitimate autonomy of local congregations, dioceses, provinces, and episcopal conferences. Each one should be permitted an appropriate scope of freedom of decision and action and be assisted "from above" only when necessary.

Evolution along this path of synodality calls for a strengthening of the Synod of Bishops, conferences of bishops, diocesan pastoral councils, and parish councils. Lay voices should be heard in every one of these venues. But we must never lose sight of the unity of the church at every level. Our unity is in our communion, the gift of the Holy Spirit, and it must always be fostered and safeguarded. The legitimate scope and freedom of discernment and action at every level must never jeopardize the unity of the body of Christ.

Diversity within Unity

The unity of the church, as vitally important as it is, does not require uniformity of discipline. The church, as it grew and spread from its origins in the Judeo-Greco-Roman world, encountered many other peoples and cultures. In the middle of the first millennium the church evangelized the Franks, Visigoths, Lombards, and Celts, among others, and later the Polish and Slavic peoples, and then the Magyars, Bohemians, and Scandinavians. In the sixteenth and seventeenth centuries the missionaries reached out to the peoples of the "new" worlds of Africa, Asia, and America. In each instance there were attempts to relate to the language and culture of the people, a process called *inculturation*. In some cases local practices were successfully adapted and adopted by the church to accommodate indigenous populations. In some cases inculturation failed.

An example of a colossal failure to inculturate successfully was the Chinese rites controversy in the seventeenth and eighteenth centuries. Jesuit missionaries, led by Matteo Ricci, a scientist and humanist, entered China in 1601. They allowed their converts to continue practicing Confucian and ancestral rites, judging them to be civil and social practices, not forms of idolatry—things like reverencing and offerings sacrifices at home shrines commemorating their deceased. They also used Chinese sacred language terms for heaven and for God (the Supreme

Lord). When other Catholic missionaries arrived in the 1630s, they were appalled at these practices and labeled them religious syncretism. The matter was referred to the Roman Curia, whence a negative judgment was issued in 1645. Upon appeal, the judgment was modified in 1656, and three years later an instruction from the Propagation of the Faith (the congregation charged with supporting and coordinating missionary activity) seemed quite open to these accommodations. Divergent reactions from missionaries led to papal decisions in 1704 and 1715 that denied the legitimacy of the adapted rites because of their "superstitious character." Finally, Pope Benedict XIV in 1742 proscribed the rites and ordered missionaries to swear an oath to obey his ruling. Some judge that the subsequent decline in success of Chinese missionary efforts was due in large part to this decision. In 1939, Pope Pius XII declared that the Confucian and ancestral practices were essentially social in nature and therefore "licit and commendable" practices.

The Catholic communion became conscious of being a world church in the latter part of the twentieth century. Its identity as a world church means more than its global extension, a presence in all parts of the world. It means that it is inculturated in all areas of the globe, engaged in dialogue with the world's diverse cultures, consciously and reciprocally influencing and being influenced by those cultures. The 1985 Synod of Bishops described *inculturation* this way: "[Inculturation] means the intimate transformation of authentic cultural values through their integration in Christianity and the insertion of Christianity in the various human cultures."

In 1990, Pope John Paul II, in his encyclical letter *Redemptoris missio (On the Permanent Validity of the Church's Missionary Mandate)*, described inculturation in the context of missionary activity:

> Through inculturation the Church makes the gospel incarnate in different cultures and at the same time introduces peoples, together with their cultures, into her own community. She transmits to them her own values, at the same time taking the good elements which already exist in them and renewing them from within. (*RM*, no. 52)

This inculturation is the activity of local churches affecting various sectors of Christian life such as worship, theology, charitable works, and church renewal. This requires a zone of freedom within which local churches can make such adaptations.

This tradition of diversity of discipline and practice alongside unity of doctrine and worship is perfectly legitimate and even most desirable, given the nature of a worldwide church that has encountered many different cultures. Christianity has never required a homogenization of cultures, though for a long time its missionary activity resembled a European religious export. Still, the church's engagement with different cultures has not been without its tensions and points of friction. At the 1998 Episcopal Synod for Asia the bishops called inculturation a major missionary challenge. They called for churches with Asian faces and voices.

What are the limits on diversity in the church? The Second Vatican Council, in *Unitatis redintegratio (Decree on Ecumenism),* offered this formula in the context of ecumenism:

> All in the church must preserve unity in essentials. But let all, according to the gifts they have received, maintain a proper freedom in their various forms of spiritual life and discipline, in their different liturgical rites, and even in their theological elaborations of revealed truth. In all thing let charity prevail. (*UR*, no. 4)

There is a Latin aphorism that epitomizes the above: *in necessariis unitas, in dubiis libertas, in omnibus caritas* (in essential matters, unity; in nonessentials, freedom; in all things, charity).

Inculturation and the resulting diversity of discipline enable the faithful to practice their faith in ways familiar to them, with their own traditions and not in ways that are foreign to them. To preserve and increase regional diversity there is an urgent need for mechanisms to achieve regional adaptation. The ancient and medieval regional councils and synods had legislative authority and decided many matters of local practice, for example, modes of receiving communion, clerical celibacy or marriage, election of bishops, and territorial or personal parishes. In the nineteenth century the provincial and plenary councils of Baltimore exercised similar decision-making functions in the United States and had great influence, for instance, in the emphasis on Catholic schools in parishes.

Going forward, there is need for new or modified structures of regional decision making. There is the possibility of regional "special" synods of bishops, for strengthened conferences of bishops, for provincial and plenary councils, with ample lay participation at every level. Checks and balances will be necessary to assure that unity in essentials is maintained and to keep local groups from losing focus. The Holy Spirit is the principle of the church's communion, and the Spirit preserves the church in truth. The Holy Spirit is the guiding light that will lead the people of God to a proper balance between diversity and unity.

Ministry

Ministry in the Roman Catholic communion is in the midst of an evolution, a change so sweeping that it may be the greatest reconfiguration of ministries since the fourth century. At that time there was an upward absorption of many diverse ministries into the role of the presbyter-pastor, who became a virtual *factotum,* one who "does it all." This left large numbers of those with lesser ministries in the role of passive participants, recipients of ministry rather than active sharers in it.

Now that process is being reversed, thanks mainly to the impetus from the Second Vatican Council's call for the active participation of all of the baptized in the life of the church. The specific elements that are causing the change are (1) the desire of parishioners, now better educated and more sophisticated, for a wider range of services and ministries in local parishes; (2) the successful participation of the laity (mostly lay women) in ministry, both volunteer and professional; (3) the revival and dramatic growth of the permanent diaconate; (4) the decline in membership in religious communities of women and men; and (5) the persistent decline in candidates for the celibate priesthood. (Some supporting statistics for the United States are shown in Figure 5-1.)

United States Religious Personnel Statistics		
	1965	**2016**
Religious sisters	179,954	47,170
Religious brothers	12,271	4,119
Permanent deacons	0	18,173
Diocesan priests	35,925	25,760
Religious priests	22,707	11,432
Parishes without a resident priest	549	3,499
	1990	**2005**
Lay parish ministers*	21,569	30,632

*working at least twenty hours a week in paid positions.

Sources: *The CARA Report* 22, no. 1 (summer 2016); David DeLambo, *Lay Parish Ministers* (New York: National Pastoral Life Center, 2005).

Figure 5-1

The theology guiding this evolution of ministry starts with ecclesiology, the nature and mission of the church and the ministries required within it, rather than starting with the sacrament of orders and relating all other ministries to that of the ordained. The ecclesiology is that of communion, local eucharistic communities bonded with one another in a sacred union, reflecting the unity of the persons in the Trinity. These local congregations of disciples—those baptized, confirmed, and receiving holy communion—are joined together in service to the church's mission in the world, a mission that carries on the mission of Jesus Christ and the Holy Spirit.

Ministries, in this vision, are organized within the common matrix of the Christian faithful, the one people of God who share in the one priesthood of Christ, both the baptized and the ordained. These ministers, ordained and lay, assume new relationships to the communities they serve when they are ordained, installed, or commissioned. They are *repositioned* within the church and in relationship to its other ministers in service to the inner life of the church and to its mission to the world.

Ministers can be distinguished into three categories within a united *ministerium* or ministerial cadre:

- *Ordained:* bishop, presbyter, deacon. Universally recognized, historic (back to the New Testament), long period of formation, permanent, laying on of hands, canonical mission.
- *Installed:* for example, pastoral associate, director of religious education. Regional standards, stable, extensive formation, formal recognition and authorization.
- *Commissioned:* for instance, lector, cantor, eucharistic minister. Local, less permanent, some formation, authorization ritual.

The diocesan bishop is the center and coordinator of ministry within the diocese. He is charged to organize, encourage, and oversee ministries, either personally or through the pastors.

This theology of ministry must be worked out according to the actual needs, resources, and conditions "on the ground": parishes closing, merging, or clustering; fewer priests; more deacons; lay ministers or deacons taking charge of parishes; and new kinds of coordination and collaboration, including shared resources, among parishes.

The shortage of priests—which is not equally shared in all parts of the world—could be solved in the United States by admitting married men to the priesthood. This is not a doctrinal matter, but rather a policy—of long standing in the Latin church—but one which has seen exceptions, both ancient and recent. The policy, which is causing a serious eucharistic shortage, could change, and it will change, but it is one of those rules that should be changed only when the people and culture of the region desire it.

The same is true of women in ministry—at all levels. Women have excelled in a wide variety of ministerial roles and in great numbers for many years. Their exclusion from the sacrament of orders is of very long standing—many centuries. Recent popes have elevated the canonical rule to a matter of doctrine, claiming that the church cannot change it, because, they argue, it was founded on the written word of God, constantly preserved in the tradition of the church, and set forth infallibly by the ordinary and universal magisterium (all the bishops in the world). However, there are serious doubts regarding the nature of the authority of this teaching and the grounds for it in the tradition. In my view, eventually the rule will change, but again, only where the people of God (under the guidance of the Holy Spirit) and their local culture are willing and receptive.

Selection of Bishops

The office of diocesan bishop is key to the church's ministerial structure, ancient or modern, and it will probably continue to be in the foreseeable future. Not only is the bishop the center and coordinator of ministries in the diocese, but he is in charge of its pastoral care, the promoter of the proper celebration of the sacraments, a prominent preacher and teacher, and the administrator of the diocese and its properties, with full legislative, executive, and judicial power. It is an awesome and challenging role that calls for presbyters who are well formed, with a genuine spirituality, endowed with solid faith, good morals, piety, zeal, wisdom, prudence, and qualities suiting them for the diocese in question. The issue is how such candidates are selected.

The church has used many procedures for the selection of its bishops through the centuries. The earliest was election of the bishop by the clergy and people of the local church. This pattern endured for the first several centuries, longer in the West than in the East, but in varied configurations, involving the metropolitan, neighboring bishops, and eventually the bishop of Rome. The office of bishop, as the church grew and spread, became more distant from the local community and closer to the local lords and princes, with the bishop an important figure in terms of finance and influence. Hence, the secular rulers took increasing control over the selection of bishops, who were then confirmed by the metropolitan, or in some instances, by the pope. In the eleventh and twelfth centuries the pope struggled to regain control of the episcopal selection process, freeing it from laity, not the lay people of the local churches, but the lay kings, princes, and lords of the land. The chaos of feudalism and the fractured societies of the Middle Ages occasioned the further separation of the bishop from the local community that had previously selected him.

At the Council of Trent in the sixteenth century (the reform council following the Protestant Reformation) the council fathers debated the three methods for selecting bishops then in force, nomination by the king, election by the cathedral chapter (leading clerics of the diocese), and papal appointment. They had problems with all three, and some suggested going back to the old tradition of local election by clergy and people. But they concluded that was untried and too risky, so they kept things as they were, employing all three methods.

In the next three hundred years, until the mid-nineteenth century, most bishops were appointed by kings and other civil rulers and confirmed by the pope. Most cathedral chapters had lost the prerogative of election, and direct papal appointment was limited to two dozen dioceses. All that changed in mid-nineteenth century when universal direct papal appointment began. Since that time nearly all bishops receive their appointments directly from the pope.

In the young church in the United States, the first bishop was elected by the missionary clerics in 1789, but subsequently he recommended other episcopal candidates to Rome without consulting the clergy, and Rome appointed some and not others. During the nineteenth century serious attempts were made to give diocesan priests a voice in the selection of their bishops when there was a vacancy, but they were not successful until the Plenary Council of Baltimore in 1884. The council decreed that, when there was an episcopal vacancy, the diocesan consultors and permanent pastors of the diocese should meet and select three candidates whose names would be forwarded to the bishops of the province, who would consider them before sending their three names to Rome. There was no discussion of consulting lay people in this process.

In 1916 the procedure was revised by the Roman Congregation for Bishops, a department of the Roman Curia, so that every other year bishops were to send the names of one or two priests they considered suitable candidates for the episcopacy to their metropolitan (the archbishop of the province). In preparing for the submission the bishop was to consult the diocesan consultors and permanent pastors, but individually and under the obligation of secrecy, not gathered in groups. The bishop could consult lay men in this process but was not required to. The bishop was not to disclose his selections to anyone except his brother bishops. After Easter, the metropolitan was to meet with the bishops of the province to discuss the candidates and to vote, in secrecy, on their preferences. The resulting list of recommended priests was sent to the Congregation for Bishops in Rome through the apostolic delegate. This entire process took place before there were any vacancies in the province. It was intended to maintain a current file of names in Rome for possible bishops when openings did occur. At which times, when a vacancy was being filled, any bishop was welcome to write to the Congregation for Bishops or to the pope with his own recommendation.

In 1972 Rome again modified the process for the selection of bishops but retained compiling the list of candidates, in secrecy, in each province every three years and forwarding it to Rome. It added another process for the supplying of candidates for an actual diocesan vacancy, but this time the burden of collecting suggestions and drawing up a list of three names to be sent to the Congregation for Bishops in Rome fell to the pontifical legate (in the United States, the papal nuncio). In the process of gathering candidates the nuncio was to contact for recommendations the metropolitan and the other diocesan bishops of the province where the vacancy had occurred as well as the president of the conference of bishops. He could also add his own recommendation.

But the papal nuncio was also required to hear some members of the diocesan consultors of the diocese in question, and he could (but need not) consult other priests of the diocese, both secular and religious, and wise lay persons. This process was incorporated into the 1983 Code of Canon Law (canon 377). Some say that these extensive consultations do not actually take place, even at the level of the bishops of the province of the vacant diocese.

Another path to becoming a bishop is less formal but often practiced. Canon 377 of the Code of Canon Law includes a simple process for the appointment of an auxiliary (or "helper") bishop. The diocesan bishop is to send the names of three priests whom he considers suitable for the office to the Congregation of Bishops. He need not consult with anyone, even neighboring bishops or his own presbyteral council. This straightforward process for supplying "helper bishops," especially in large archdioceses like Boston, New York, Chicago, or Los Angeles is much more significant than it at first appears. These auxiliary bishops, chosen by the diocesan bishop as his helpers, are obviously men whom he favors and thinks will serve him and the diocese well. But these auxiliary bishops, after five or ten years of such service, very often desire and receive "their own diocese" somewhere else. This is a very common practice in the United States. Just one example: Boston's auxiliaries at one point ended up in dioceses in Louisiana, Ohio, Indiana, and Wisconsin. All were worthy diocesan bishops, but they were not known or chosen by the churches or even the neighboring bishops of the dioceses they received. Instead, they were "promoted" as a reward for their service in their previous diocese. (There is more discussion of auxiliary bishops below.)

Perhaps an even greater weakness in the process of the selection of our bishops is the personal interventions that secure episcopal appointments for friends or admired colleagues. Members of the Congregation for Bishops in Rome are in a position to exercise this kind of preference, and it is not at all uncommon for cardinals and archbishops to intervene on behalf of someone they prefer for a given vacancy, even when that priest has no relation to the diocese in question. This system of patronage *(padronanza)* has been around for a long time.

The process for the selection of bishops should evolve in the following direction:

- A greater initial involvement of the diocesan church in assessing its needs and the qualities desired in a new bishop; the diocesan pastoral council could be the focus of this prayerful effort.
- Continued engagement of the metropolitan and other bishops of the province in the suggestion of candidates.
- Greater involvement of the Conference of Bishops in evaluating candidates and selecting the three names to be forwarded to the Congregation for Bishops in Rome.
- A reduced role for the papal nuncio; he should continue as an adviser to the conference in the selection process and as a conduit for transmitting the candidates' names to Rome,

but not have the ability to make changes to the choices made by the conference. The participation of the Conference of Bishops (or a committee thereof) and the nuncio should help to overcome local prejudices, like those of ethnic or lingual groups or a majority neglect of minorities.

Auxiliary Bishops

Some larger archdioceses in our country request and receive auxiliary bishops, most often selected from among their own presbyters, for use as administrative or sacramental assistance to the archdiocesan bishop, or to represent and minister to minority groups within the local church, for insistence, ethnic, racial, or language communities. In 2015, Chicago had six auxiliary bishops; Boston and Los Angeles had five; and Philadelphia and Newark had four each.

We have already remarked on the effect that these auxiliary bishops have on the selection of diocesan bishops when they migrate to head up dioceses, unknown to them, in distant parts of the country. But there is a more serious reason why auxiliary bishops are a bad idea: they distort the vision of what a bishop is meant to be in relation to a diocese. The Second Vatican Council spent five whole pages in *Christus Dominus (Decree on the Pastoral Office of Bishops in the Church)* describing the bishop's responsibilities for his diocese. It begins this way:

A diocese is a section of the people of God whose pastoral care is entrusted to a bishop in cooperation with his priests. Thus in conjunction with their pastor and gathered by him into one flock in the Holy Spirit through the gospel and the eucharist, they constitute a particular church. In this church the one, holy, catholic and apostolic church of Christ is truly present and at work.

Individual bishops, to whom the pastoral care of particular churches has been committed, are the proper, official and immediate shepherds of these churches under the authority of the supreme pontiff. Accordingly, they feed their sheep in the name of the Lord by fulfilling their office of teaching, sanctifying and governing them. (*CD*, no. 11)

And the role of bishops is also mentioned in the *Dogmatic Constitution on the Church*:

> Individual bishops . . . are the visible principle and foundation of unity in their own particular churches:. . . (*LG,* no. 23; see also *LG,* nos. 18–27; *CD,* nos. 11–21)

Having more than one person in the diocese with the title and sacred order of the episcopate blurs the unique and traditional role of the diocesan bishop as the unifying figure in the local church.

It used to be that only a bishop could give the sacrament of confirmation, and assistant bishops were needed in large dioceses to help with confirmations, but the liturgical law has been changed so that the diocesan bishop can grant the faculty to confirm to one or more presbyters. Hence, the pressure on the diocesan bishop is lessened, and the need for "helper" bishops to assist with confirmations has been removed.

The other reason for auxiliary bishops in large archdioceses is for each one of them to serve as a regional administrator for a geographical area of the archdiocese, often called a vicariate or deanery. But these regional coordinators are not required to be bishops. Canon law has long provided for such regional leaders to be presbyters called deans or vicars forane. The 1983 Code of Canon Law provided for the office of "episcopal vicar" to exercise authority over a specific part of the diocese or a certain area of pastoral ministry. They are not bishops and have no need for the episcopal order or title.

Another problem, somewhat related to the role of auxiliary bishop, is the practice of transferring bishops, sometimes three or four times, from one diocese to another, most often from a small or remote diocese to a larger, more prosperous, urban diocese. Sometimes these transfers are necessary because of special problems or "bad fits" between bishop and people, but most often they are seen as promotions or rewards. Often small dioceses receive a bishop from another area, and he moves on after three or five years, and someone else comes in. These dioceses are made to feel like way stations or training grounds to some place "better" rather than as a unique portion of the people of God with a dedicated leader. In the early church such transfers were seen as causes of "great disturbance" and explicitly forbidden (Council of Nicaea, a. 325). These are different times, but diocesan bishops ought not be treated like managers of local franchises or regional factories of a worldwide conglomerate. These men are not mere administrators or caretakers of an office. They are shepherds who have been entrusted with the care of their people. As Paul said in his farewell to the elders of the church at Ephesus:

> Keep watch over yourselves and over the flock, of which the Holy Spirit has made you overseers, to shepherd the church of God that he obtained with the blood of his own Son. (Acts 20:28)

Chapter 6

Evolution of the Sacraments

Sacraments are encounters with Christ and the Holy Spirit, and they are actions and prayers of the church. The following three examples—marriage, penance, and anointing of the sick—show how sacraments evolve. The church, one portion of the people of God, has changed sacramental teachings and practices many times in the past and continues to do so. These three are instances that are in need of further change.

The process of sacramental change is not always progress, not always a smooth trajectory of improvement. It is subject to the tug and pull of its contexts: the historical moment, the surrounding culture, and the understanding of the human person.

Marriage: An Intimate Community of Life and Love

Marriage, thought to be one of the most stable elements in human societies, has evolved and continues to evolve, sometimes at a startlingly rapid rate. There were times when polygamy was an accepted practice. Arranged marriages—for political or financial purposes rather than because of romantic attraction—are still common in some places. Couples are marrying later, if at all. Cohabitation is increasingly accepted; many more children are born out of wedlock. Marriage equality, to the extent that it has been achieved, has only recently arrived. And recently, with amazing swiftness, same-sex marriage has found acceptance in North America. And divorce, once rare and socially unacceptable, is now frequent and no longer stigmatized. Marriage in North America is in a situation of crisis.

The Old Testament spoke of divinely sanctioned polygamy, concubinage, and divorce, as well as the mythic union of Adam and Eve. Jesus was caught up in the debate over "easy divorce" in his own time, causing him to argue:

> Some Pharisees came, and to test him they asked, "Is it lawful for a man to divorce his wife?" He answered them, "What did Moses command you?" They said, "Moses allowed a man to write a certificate of dismissal and to divorce her." But Jesus said to them, "Because of your hardness of heart he wrote this commandment for you. But from the beginning of creation, 'God made them male and female. For this reason a man shall leave his father and mother and be joined to his wife, and the two shall become one flesh.' So they are no longer two, but one flesh. Therefore what God has joined together, let no one separate." (Mark 10:2–9)

In the context of this citation and those in the Gospels of Matthew and Luke, it is clear that Jesus was not speaking of a legal or moral norm; rather, he was speaking prophetically of the radical demands of the reign of God. He evoked in his followers a commitment to live differently because of God's future reign drawn near. To live in the reign of God entailed restoring the relationships of all creatures to the plan of God the creator, hence Jesus's quotation of Genesis.

Soon the early Christian communities, becoming aware that the reign of God was not imminent, began to come to terms with the lived reality of marriage. Paul's letter to the church at Corinth makes an exception in the case of a "mixed marriage" (a Christian and a nonbeliever); if the unbeliever separates, the believer is not bound. "It is to peace that God has called you" (1 Cor 7:12–15). Matthew's Gospel inserts the exception of unchastity in the general prohibition of divorce (Matt 5:32; 19:9). Those early communities faced the human reality of broken marriages in their midst.

Marriage existed long before the Christian church, and the church's encounter with the institution of marriage was varied and historically conditioned. This brief narrative of the (Western) church's encounter with marriage is told in chronological stages, sometimes overlapping and cumulative—successive stages add to the previous ones.

In the first three centuries the church preached about marriage in terms of morality and pastoral care. But marriage was a *secular* reality, a family affair, experienced by the baptized "in the Lord" (1 Cor 7:39; Col 3:18), but governed by the laws of the Roman Empire and local customs. After the conversion of northern tribes, Germanic and Frankish, their rules or customs were accepted by the church. From the fourth through the tenth centuries the church gradually developed liturgical rituals in which the bishop or priest was present to bless the spouses at their home. Marriages began to take place in churches in the fifth century, but a nuptial eucharist was not commonly celebrated until after the year 1000.

In the ninth and tenth centuries the church began to assume some responsibility for marriages, like confirming that the spouses were not already married or related within forbidden degrees of kinship, publicly witnessing the exchange of consent, and making a record of its occurrence. These secular functions became canonical requirements. Up to this point the church acknowledged the jurisdiction of the secular authorities over marriage, concluded within the family in accord with tribal customs. Pope Nicholas I (858–67) decided that a marriage was valid, even if all the ceremonies surrounding the wedding were neglected, as long as the baptized couple gave mutual consent.

In the course of the ninth to twelfth centuries the church assumed jurisdiction over marriage, because of the weakened power of kings and the tumult of the feudal times. It made the rules for entering into marriage as well as adjudicating its validity in disputed cases. It was only after this assumption of juridical authority over marriage that theologians began to speak of marriage as a *sacrament*, or sacred sign that conferred grace, in the eleventh to thirteenth centuries.

Marriage was officially referred to as a sacrament for the first time in a local synod in Verona (1184), and listed as one of the seven sacraments at the Council of Lyons (1274) and the Council of Florence (1439). This position was emphatically affirmed by the Council of Trent (1563), which added the requirement that marriages between baptized Christians must be celebrated before a priest and two or three witnesses in order to be valid; this was to combat the abuse of clandestine (unwitnessed) marriages that could be later denied and abandoned. (This rule of "canonical form" for the validity of marriages was not applied universally until 1908.)

In the eighteenth and nineteenth centuries the church struggled to maintain its control over the sacrament of matrimony while conceding to civil authority the civil effects of the marriage contract.

The foregoing narrative of the church's long and varied encounter with marriage is inserted here to emphasize the diverse attitudes and regulations the church has employed through the centuries in its attempts to honor and preserve marriage as the sign of Christ's love for his church (Eph 5:25) and to support married couples and their families. The church's teaching and practices regarding marriage have evolved and will continue to evolve.

For example, the regulation from the Council of Trent regarding the (then) real problem of clandestine marriages—that every baptized Catholic must be married by an authorized priest and two or three witnesses for their marriage to be canonically valid—is now pastorally counterproductive. A large number of baptized Catholics today do not get married in the church, for whatever reasons, and as a result their marriages are canonically invalid. It is relatively easy for them to have their marriages declared null by the church should they so desire. Canon law should be changed to encourage Catholics to marry in the church, but not at the penalty of invalidity if they choose not to do so.

Catholic Church *teaching* on marriage and family has developed radically over the years, and the changes introduced at the Second Vatican Council (1962–65) were major, for example, the use of covenant language for marriage in place of contract language, the revision of the ends of marriage, and the description of marriage as an intimate sharing of life and love.

The church's *discipline* of marriage has also changed considerably since the council; for example, mixed marriage with another Christian is no longer an impediment and may be celebrated in church, declarations of nullity for lack of canonical form may be granted by the person preparing the couple for marriage (rather than referred to a diocesan official), annulments of marriages are frequently granted on psychological grounds, and lay judges and defenders of the bond, themselves married, are frequently part of the tribunal process.

In the face of a "marriage crisis," the church needs to rethink and reconfigure its ministry to married persons (including cohabiting couples, those civilly married, the divorced and remarried, and those in same-sex unions) so that it is multifaceted and flexible. The church's main concern is threefold: (1) to support and encourage permanence and fidelity within marriage, (2) to assist couples toward success and happiness in their married lives, and (3) to give spiritual support and pastoral reconciliation to those who have experienced the tragedy of divorce, a reconciliation that results in conversion and, ultimately, full eucharistic communion.

This process of ecclesial reconciliation should be envisioned within a larger ministry to marriage and family, one that includes effective programs of marriage preparation, support, and enrichment, as well as special assistance for troubled marriages. This comprehensive approach should be a high priority for the church in this time when marriage and families are in critical need of help and support.

This process of ecclesial reconciliation is better treated in the moral order than the juridical, that is, in the realm of moral fault, repentance, conversion, forgiveness, and reconciliation rather than in the legal order of invalidity, declaration of nullity, and convalidation. Not that the marriage tribunal, or other canonical procedures, have no place in a revised pastoral strategy. Quite the contrary. When people explicitly request a clarification of their status, for reasons of public propriety or personal conscience, then a canonical clarification should be given to them. Or when a marriage was of very short duration and there are clear grounds for nullity—for example, lack of form, prior bond, coerced consent, in other words when pastoral discretion inclines toward a juridical process as the obvious solution—then that option should be offered.

The whole pastoral approach to the reconciliation of divorced and remarried Catholics should begin with a process of discernment. When they approach the church or when the church's pastoral agents reach out to them, the first step should be a prayerful and thoughtful encounter with a "pastoral diagnostician," a knowledgeable person who can listen with sensitivity to the story of the original marriage; its failure; the process and context of the subsequent union; and the faith, commitment, and motivations of the present partners.

This pastor or pastoral agent can gently and gradually assist the couple toward the most appropriate of the options open to them. These options might include leaving them in good faith (not telling them they are living in sin), an extended examination of conscience, a prayerful process of penance (in an *ordo paenitentium*, an order of penitents like the order of catechumens preparing for baptism), access to the sacraments of reconciliation and eucharist, *or* the initiation of a canonical petition for declaration of nullity or dissolution, if that is desired and possible. Ultimately the choice, aided by the power of discretion and the grace of the Holy Spirit, should be that of the couple.

One key component of this overall strategy might be a discreet pastoral intervention when a marriage is perceived to be under stress. Is there a way for friends, mentor couples, a pastor, skilled mediators or counselors to intervene and offer assistance before differences between the spouses have hardened into intractability?

The church's pastoral concern is focused on the members of the Christian faithful—on individuals or married couples. It searches for ways to assist and support these brothers and sisters in Christ, to reach out to them with love, to warmly welcome them within the community of faith, both for their sake and for the sake of the church. The number of Catholics alienated because of divorce is staggering. This person-by-person reconciliation must remain in the forefront of pastoral action. Gospel images of the shepherd and the lost sheep, of the prodigal son and forgiving father (both in Luke 15) come to mind, as well as Jesus's words that it is the sick rather than those in good health who need a physician (Matt 9).

Pope Francis, in his rich and remarkable apostolic exhortation on love in the family *Amoris laetitia (The Joy of Love)* states this in the context of discernment of irregular marital situations:

As for the way of dealing with different "irregular" situations, the Synod Fathers reached a general consensus, which I support: "In considering a pastoral approach toward people who have contracted a civil marriage, who are divorced and remarried, or simply living together, the church has the responsibility of helping them understand the divine pedagogy of grace in their lives and offering them assistance so that they can reach the fullness of God's plan for them," something which is always possible by the power of the Holy Spirit. (*AL,* no. 297)

Penance: Conversion and Reconciliation

The risen Lord told his disciples in Jerusalem:

"Thus it is written, that the Messiah is to suffer and rise from the dead on the third day and that repentance and forgiveness of sins is to be proclaimed in his name to all nations beginning from Jerusalem." (Luke 24:46–47)

"Peace be with you. As the Father has sent me, so I send you." When he had said this, he breathed on them and said to them, "Receive the Holy Spirit. If you forgive the sins of any, they are forgiven them; if you retain the sins of any, they are retained." (John 20:21–23)

Jesus Christ brought about reconciliation between God and humankind through the mystery of his death and resurrection. The Lord entrusted this ministry of reconciliation to the church, which carries it out by baptizing in water and the Holy Spirit. Because of human weakness Christians sometimes break off their friendship with God by sinning, so the Lord instituted the sacrament of penance for the pardon of sins committed after baptism. The church has celebrated this sacrament in various forms throughout the centuries.

Indeed, the forms of the celebration of the sacrament have been so diverse through the years as to be scarcely recognizable as one and the same reality. In the New Testament communities there were actions taken against those who offended, but no liturgy of reconciliation was evident, aside from the Lord's prayer, which included a petition for forgiveness, and the greeting of peace that began eucharistic celebrations.

In the second to fourth centuries two different penitential practices developed and spread. The one, *public or canonical penance,* meant the public admission of serious sin, petition for the community's prayer, entry into a group of penitents *(ordo paenitentium),* exclusion from the eucharistic celebration, and after a considerable length of time, a grant of "peace with the church" and invocation of the Holy Spirit, a process of reconciliation. This procedure was not repeatable; it could be taken only once. Alongside this formal penitential process was a path of repentance through prayer, mortification, and good works, which ordinary sinners pursued in their everyday lives. In both situations forgiveness of sins came through the church and its prayer.

The most common form of penitential reconciliation became *penance for the dying.* Because public penance could not be repeated, the faithful often postponed reconciliation until near death, at which point they would summon the priest to minister to them by imposing hands or administering holy communion.

By the sixth and seventh centuries the usage of the order of penitents had declined, and an attenuated form of penitential reconciliation became attached to Lent and the Lenten fast, from Ash Wednesday to Holy Thursday, when the penitents would be reconciled. Lent had become a season of penitential purification in preparation for Easter communion. By the tenth century all Christians were expected to become Lenten penitents. Public (canonical) penance had long since fallen into disuse.

Celtic monks, probably influenced by Eastern monasticism, introduced into the British Isles and France the practice of *private penance* in the sixth to ninth centuries. Originated as a form of spiritual direction for those faithful living in the environs of monasteries, this practice of confession and assigned penances found fertile soil in the church, in which canonical penance had radically declined. The monks, not always ordained, would hear and counsel penitents and then assign them a specific penance, often using penitential books to ascertain what form and length of penance was appropriate for particular sins.

Bishops in France originally opposed this development, since they and their communities had no part in it, but it answered a pastoral need and continued to spread. In the ninth century the bishops reached a compromise: public penance was to be done for grave sins that were publicly known, but private penance sufficed for sins that were not public knowledge. Confessors were limited to ordained priests, confession and assignment of penance could be repeated, and the result was access to holy communion.

Two other communal forms of the sacrament at this time call for brief mention. One was the practice of *solemn penance* associated with the season of Lent. It called for the public penitents to be expelled from the community at the beginning of Lent, after receiving ashes, being clothed with penitential garb, and entering into a fast. The bishop reconciled them on Holy Thursday by praying over them and admitting them to communion. Another form, *general absolution,* was a recognized communal penitential liturgy in use from the ninth to the fourteenth centuries. It was usually in the context of a eucharistic celebration (often during Holy Week) and consisted of a liturgy of the word, an examination of conscience, a general confession, and absolution given collectively to those who wished it.

From the tenth century to the twelfth, private penance became increasingly prominent, while other forms of penance declined. Oral private confession was followed by absolution (pardon or remission), with the satisfaction (assigned penance) following afterward. The indicative pronouncement of absolution by the priest ("I absolve you . . .") gave the assurance of divine forgiveness. Then the Fourth Lateran Council (1215) made it an obligation for all those over the age of discretion to make a confession every year to their own parish priest in preparation for their Easter communion. This strong endorsement of private confession virtually eliminated all interest in any other form of the sacrament of penance. By the thirteenth century penance was almost totally a private act. The priest's absolution, an exercise of the "power of the keys," was the only ecclesial element.

The actions of the Council of Trent (1551), in response to the Protestant reformers who rejected auricular confession, forcefully reaffirmed the decisions of the Fourth Lateran Council and gave theological explanations for each of the elements of the sacrament: contrition, confession, satisfaction, and priestly absolution. Moreover, it stated that the institution of sacramental confession and its necessity for salvation are of divine law. The die was cast for the sacrament for the next four hundred years. (Although the official liturgical reform books after the Council of Trent—the *Pontificale* (1596) and the *Rituale* (1614)—included ceremonies for solemn penance, it seems they were very seldom used.)

It wasn't until the liturgical renewal sparked by the Second Vatican Council that a reform of the sacrament of penance was initiated. The post-conciliar drafting of a new ritual for penance was delayed for several years because of sharp differences of opinion relating to Trent's insistence on integral confession and the priest's judicial absolution, and the contemporary increased use of communal penance celebrations with general absolution. The reformed *Rite of Penance* was issued in 1974 and contained three distinct forms of sacramental rituals:

1. *For reconciling individual penitents:* Priest and penitent are face to face or behind a screen in a reconciliation room. The ritual begins with a welcoming greeting, a sign of the cross, an invitation to trust in God, a reading of the word of God, confession and acceptance of penance, penitent's prayer of sorrow, absolution (delivered with priest's hand extended over penitent's head), praise of God and dismissal.

2. *For reconciling several penitents with individual confession and absolution:* The community gathers in church or chapel. The rite begins with a song, greeting, and opening prayer; then a reading of the word of God; homily; examination of conscience; general confession of sins; prayers for forgiveness; individual confessions; absolution; acceptance of penance (with several priests, separately); proclamation of praise for God's mercy; concluding prayer of thanksgiving; blessing; and dismissal.

3. *For reconciling several penitents with general confession and absolution:* Everything is the same as in number 2 above except for an instruction to repent and turn away from sin; to confess individually at the proper time any serious sins that cannot be confessed here; and a gesture to show desire for absolution (kneeling, bowing head).

The two communal forms of the sacrament highlight the church and its local community as the place of conversion and reconciliation, restoring to the sacrament an ecclesial and social sense, while the private form maintains the possibility of interpersonal dialogue between the penitent and priest as spiritual guide.

The serious shortcoming in the rite is the severe restriction placed on the use of the third form of the sacrament because of the omission of individual confession and the reluctance to permit the use of general absolution. The 1983 Code of Canon Law limits the use of general absolution to imminent danger of death or grave necessity, that is, too many penitents and not enough confessors to hear their confessions properly, so that the penitents are deprived of sacramental grace or holy communion for a long while. The diocesan bishop is to decide whether those conditions are fulfilled. When the pastoral practice of the third form with general absolution became more common in United States dioceses, the Roman Curia resistance was strong and sustained. Bishops were ordered not to allow the practice of general absolution.

The use of the sacrament of penance has declined drastically in the United States over the last fifty years. The 1972 Rite of Penance did not succeed in reversing this negative trend, despite considerable efforts. Changes must be made to permit wider use of the third form of the rite; that is, general confession of sins and general absolution can and should be permitted in normal communal celebrations of the sacrament, not restricted to the "danger of death or grave necessity." The first form, private confession, should be maintained and nurtured, depending on penitents' needs and the availability of priests skilled in the formation of Christian conscience.

The creation of a new structure of reconciliation, a fourth form of the sacrament, a modern order of penitents, parallel to the Rite for the Christian Initiation of Adults, has been recommended for those baptized who have never been catechized, or who are converting to the church, or who have fallen away and are returning. The local community could guide a process of ongoing conversion that would include spiritual direction, community prayer, catechesis, a celebration of the ritual of reconciliation, and an ongoing support group. This form was proposed by Cardinal Bernardin at the 1983 Synod of Bishops, which had as its theme "Reconciliation and Penance in the Mission of the Church.")

Our radical need is for a penitent church, a reconciled and reconciling community that can mediate the experience of a merciful, compassionate, and loving God. The Holy Spirit has helped to form and reform the church's penitential ministries of conversion and reconciliation through the ages. The Spirit is present today to help us breathe new life into the sacrament and the reality of conversion and reconciliation.

Anointing of the Sick:
The Grace of the Holy Spirit for Healing and Strength

What we know as the sacrament of anointing of the sick is alluded to in the Gospel of Mark, when Jesus was teaching in the villages of Galilee:

> He called the twelve and began to send them out two by two, and gave them authority over the unclean spirits. . . . So they went out and proclaimed that all should repent. They cast out many demons, and anointed with oil many who were sick and cured them. (Mark 6:7, 12–13)

The letter of James, one of the so-called catholic epistles (directed to the universal church rather than to a particular church), describes the appropriately Christian response to sickness:

> Are any among you sick? They should call for the elders of the church and have them pray over them, anointing them with oil in the name of the Lord. The prayer of faith will save the sick, and the Lord will raise them up; and anyone who has committed sins will be forgiven. (Jas 5:14–15)

"Elders of the church" means those in an official position in the local church, not those advanced in age. The text, using the words "raise them up," the same expression that described Jesus's healing of Simon's mother-in-law (Mark 1:31) and the boy afflicted with seizures (Mark 9:27), refers to a restoration to health for the sick person as well as to the forgiveness of sins.

The early church made use of this ministry to the sick for several centuries before liturgical rituals were developed in the eighth century. Much earlier, there were fixed formulas for the blessing of oil used in the sacrament. Pope Innocent I (417), in a letter to a bishop, stated that bishops as well as priests *(sacerdotes)* could use this oil in anointing the sick, but so could members of the Christian faithful. The consecrated oil was often used by the faithful for themselves or their families when they were sick. This was apparently considered what we would call a *sacramental* as over against what would become known as a *sacrament* administered by a priest or bishop. For instance, Caesarius, bishop of Arles (502–42), warned his people not to resort to pagan practices in times of sickness, but said rather:

> How much more right and salutary it would be if they made haste to the church . . . and piously anointed themselves and their families with holy oil; and in accordance with the words of the Apostle James received not only health of body but also pardon of their sins. (Serm. 279, 5 *Patrologia Latina*, 39, 2273)

This form of private anointing was more convenient; priests would be summoned only in the event of more grave sickness.

In the ninth century the Carolingian reform emphasized the administration of the sacrament of anointing, even as its practice waned. Its decline may have been the result of prohibiting any use of blessed oil by non-priests, together with the custom of remunerating priests for their ministry to the sick. This placed a burden on poor people.

Anointing became associated with the sacrament of penance. It was seen as a completion of a penitential rite that carried with it the expectation of a changed lifestyle, a conversion of life to a permanent penitential state, implying, for example, abstinence from marital intercourse and from the eating of flesh meat. This misguided belief, which the church constantly tried to correct, caused anointing to be avoided or postponed to near death. Also, anointing was linked to *viaticum* (holy communion as "food for the journey" into the next life). This too caused it to be associated with the end of life. The rite became known as extreme unction (last anointing), a sacrament for the dying. This impression and this label endured until the Second Vatican Council despite efforts of more recent catechisms and papal writings that reasserted anointing as a sacrament for the sick.

The Council of Trent (1551), which was reacting to the Protestant reformers who denied that the anointing described in the letter of James was a sacrament, strongly reaffirmed the sacrament of anointing. It declared that the effect of the sacrament was the grace of the Holy Spirit that takes away sins, comforts and strengthens the soul of the sick person by arousing in him or her great trust in divine mercy, and helps the person bear the trials of the illness. The council said that "the elders of the church" that James spoke of meant "bishops or priests *(sacerdotes)* duly ordained by them," and that only priests are the proper ministers of anointing.

The Second Vatican Council, in its sweeping renewal of the church's liturgical life, explicitly called for changing the name of the sacrament of anointing from extreme unction to anointing of the sick, making clear that it was not intended for the end of life but for those who are seriously ill at any stage of life. The council did not restate that only priests were the proper ministers of the sacrament, but the post-conciliar document containing the revised rites, *Pastoral Care of the Sick: Rites of Anointing and Viaticum*, restricts its administration to ordained priests or bishops.

Communal anointing services for the sick are now celebrated in parishes, hospitals, and retirement homes on a regular basis several times a year, often within the context of the Eucharist, to great pastoral success. Such services allow deacons and lay ministers to conduct parts of the celebrations but not to perform the anointing themselves. In this time of shortage of priests, it is imperative that others in addition to priests be permitted to administer the sacrament of anointing for the benefit of the faithful in need, both in communal settings and to individuals at home or in hospital. Especially permanent deacons (who now number approximately eighteen thousand in the United States, many hospital chaplains) should be enabled to perform this ministry, as they ably perform many other ministries, including the anointing at baptisms. There are recent precedents for the extension of the presiding ministry in other sacraments; for instance, priests now confer the sacrament of confirmation on adult converts. Some lay ministers, like pastoral associates and chaplains, should also be admitted to this ministry of anointing, where priests are not available. *Sacramenta propter homines* (sacraments are for the people) is an ancient adage. It should be applied here to give more of the faithful access to the sacrament of the anointing of the sick.

Further Directions

These ruminations suggest other areas in which the contemporary church needs to further evolve. In addition to the structural developments outlined in Chapter 5 and the evolution of the sacraments in Chapter 6, these three additional facets of the church's life need review and development

1. the teaching function,
2. ecological concerns, and
3. relations with other churches and religions.

Some brief suggestions follow.

Teaching Function

Christ has entrusted the church with the task of proclaiming God's revealed truth, with the assistance of the Holy Spirit, by all the means available, from preaching and catechesis to universities and the various media.

The field of communications is in a revolutionary mode. The church needs to reassess its ways and means of messaging the good news. This includes the media that are used—print versus visual, electronic, digital; the languages and images that are employed, and the process of formulating the message. Some parts of the church are well advanced and sophisticated in these areas of communications, and some are still stuck in old-fashioned modes.

When it comes to consultation in the process of preparing pastoral statements, the United States Conference of Catholic Bishops achieved two stellar successes back in the 1980s. It held hearings all over the country and listened to a wide spectrum of opinions—mainly of lay persons, often experts—before attempting to formulate its documents. The results were two excellent treatises: *The Challenge of Peace: God's Promise and Our Response, A Pastoral Letter on War and Peace* (1983) and *Economic Justice for All: Pastoral Letter on Catholic Social Teaching and the US Economy* (1986).

The Vatican criticized the bishops' procedure in preparing these documents; the bishops, it said, listened too much and taught too little! The process has not been repeated.

Another project, much more modest but also quite successful, was *Follow the Way of Love: US Bishops' Pastoral Message to Families* (1993), a letter prepared for the Year of the Family in 1994. It was written with realistic language and lifelike images mainly by married men and women.

There are numerous examples, both good and bad, of church communications at every level—parish, diocese, national, and international. Our communications need to be the most effective that we can afford.

Pope Francis has issued two remarkable teaching documents: *Evangelii gaudium (On the Proclamation of the Gospel in Today's World)* and *Amoris laetitia (The Joy of Love: On Love in the Family)*. Although lengthy, they are examples of the carefully crafted, rich resources available for all those who take part in the church's teaching function, whether officially or personally.

Ecology

Pope Francis's most solemn teaching document, the encyclical letter *Laudato Si' (On Care for Our Common Home)* (2015) raises and explores ecology, an issue of vital importance for a church with its eye fixed on the reign of God. His intended audience is not just the church but all of humankind, who share our common home and who have used and abused it as its lords and masters.

The pope draws attention to the immensity and urgency of the present ecological crisis confronting the world, its many facets and root causes, and the principles from the Judeo-Christian tradition that can help the human family deal with the crisis. He proposes dialogues and actions on the international scale, like accords on climate control, as well as on the plane of individuals, like carpooling or turning off unnecessary lights. He reminds us that "everything is connected" (LS, no. 117); concern for our environment is joined to our love for our fellow human beings and our commitment to solving the problems of society. He urges an ecological conversion leading to a pervasive, personal, ecological spirituality that can motivate us to a passionate concern for the protection of our world.

All of creation bears the imprint of the Trinity—the Father as ultimate source of everything; the Son, united to earth in his incarnation; and the Holy Spirit, bond of love, intimately present at the very heart of the universe, inspiring and bringing new pathways. Everything is interconnected, and this invites us to develop a spirituality of global solidarity that flows from the mystery of the Trinity.

Living out our calling to be protectors of creation is essential to a life of virtue; it is not an optional or secondary aspect of our Christian experience. It must be high on the church's agenda.

Ecumenical and Interreligious Action

After his last supper with his disciples, Jesus looked up to heaven and prayed to his Father for his disciples:

> Protect them in your name that you have given me so that they may be one as we are one. . . . I ask not only on behalf of these, but also on behalf of those who will believe in me through their word, that they may all be one. As you, Father, are in me and I am in you, may they also be one in us, so that the world may believe that you have sent me. The glory that you have given me I have given them, so that they may be one as we are one, I in them and you in me, that they may become completely one. So that the world may know that you have sent me. (John 17:11, 20–23)

At the Second Vatican Council, the Catholic Church joined the ecumenical movement that strives to restore the unity among Christians for which Christ prayed. Vatican II's 1964 *Unitatis redintegratio (Decree on Ecumenism)* expressed this strong commitment and the means to achieve its end.

In 1995, Pope John Paul II, after he had been the bishop of Rome for seventeen years, issued the encyclical letter *Ut unum sint (On Commitment to Ecumenism)* reaffirming that commitment and expanding the ways to pursue it. He says that ecumenism is not some sort of "appendix" added on to the church's traditional activity; rather it is an organic part of the church's life and work and must pervade all that the church is and does. The pope reminds the whole Christian family that it is already in profound communion, and that it must continue to pray and work toward joining in a full communion, drawn from the source of perfect communion, the unity of Father, Son, and Holy Spirit.

The grace of the Holy Spirit, the ecumenical dialogues, and the thousands of interchurch cooperative projects, have brought us a long way since the Second Vatican Council, and the pope asks how much further we have to go before we can celebrate together in peace the holy Eucharist of the Lord. Christ ardently desires the full and visible communion of all those communities in which his Spirit dwells.

Among the steps along the way, the pope says:

> I am convinced that I have a particular responsibility in this regard . . . to find a way of exercising the primacy [the Petrine office], which, while in no way renouncing what is essential to its mission, is nonetheless open to a new situation." (*Uus,* no. 95)

He invites the leaders of other Christian churches to join with him in a patient and friendly dialogue on this issue, while listening only to what Christ wills for his church, "that they all may be one." There has been no announced result of this dialogue, but Pope Francis appears to be reshaping the primacy in some ways, at least in style and operation.

"There is no doubt that the Holy Spirit is active in this endeavor [the ecumenical movement] and that he is leading the church to the full realization of the Father's plan, in conformity with the will of Christ" (*Uus,* no. 100). Still, there is much unfinished business in the whole ecumenical project, and it must be pursued vigorously.

The dialogue and cooperation among the various *world religions*, in addition to the ecumenical efforts toward *Christian* unity, was also recognized and fostered at the Second Vatican Council, especially in its 1965 document *Nostra aetate (Declaration on the Church's Relation to Non-Christian Religions)*. It specifically mentioned Hinduism and Buddhism, Muslims and Jews, as worthy of respect and urged the preservation and promotion of the spiritual and moral goods and social values found among them. The document condemned as foreign to the mind of Christ any discrimination against or harassment of any people by reason of race, color, class or religion. All are children of God, members of the human family, to be treated with justice and love.

Interreligious dialogue and collaboration has become a much greater issue in the world since 1965, because of geopolitical disputes and conflicts, among other reasons. The church must attend to this area with increased involvement, sensitivity, and commitment.

In Conclusion

These final remarks are not a conclusion from or summary of all that went before. For such an overview of the book, the reader should go back to the "Introduction" or return to Chapter 4, "The People of God, the Holy Spirit, and the Reign of God." The central theme of the book is set forth there in a few pages.

The theme of this book is that the Holy Spirit has a profound influence on the life of God's people, and specifically on that portion of God's people we know as the church. The Spirit is the guiding force behind the church—its very soul. And what the Spirit is driving the church *toward*, its goal, is the reign of God proclaimed and inaugurated by Jesus of Nazareth.

God's time always includes our now. Our past, present, and future are all included in the *now* of God's time. Our moment to join the Spirit's direction toward the goal of God's reign is now.

Bibliography

Historical Sources

Burgess
Stanley Burgess, *The Holy Spirit: Ancient Christian Traditions* (Peabody, MA: Hendrickson, 1984).

Jurgens I
William Jurgens, *The Faith of the Early Fathers* (Collegeville, MN: Liturgical Press, 1970).

Jurgens II
William Jurgens, *The Faith of the Early Fathers*, vol. 2 (Collegeville, MN: Liturgical Press, 1979).

Meier II
John Meier, *A Marginal Jew: Rethinking the Historical Jesus*, vol. 2, *Mentor, Message, and Miracles* (New York: Doubleday, 1991).

Pelikan III
Jaroslav Pelikan, *The Christian Tradition: A History of the Development of Doctrine*, vol. 3, *The Growth of Medieval Theology (600–1300)* (Chicago: University of Chicago Press, 1978).

Quasten I
Johannes Quasten, *Patrology*, vol. 1, *The Beginnings of Patristic Literature* (Westminster, MD: Newman Press, 1950).

Quasten II
Johannes Quasten, *Patrology*, vol. 2, *The Ante-Nicene Literature after Irenaeus* (Westminster, MD: Newman Press, 1953).

Quasten III
Johannes Quasten, *Patrology*, vol. 3, *The Golden Age of Greek Patristic Literature* (Westminster, MD: Newman Press, 1960).

Tanner I
Norman Tanner, *Decrees of the Ecumenical Councils*, vol. 1, *Nicaea I to Lateran V* (Washington, DC: Sheed and Ward and Georgetown University Press, 1990).

Tanner II   Norman Tanner, *Decrees of the Ecumenical Councils*, vol. 2, *Trent to Vatican II* (Washington, DC: Sheed and Ward and Georgetown University Press, 1990).

Documents of the Second Vatican Council

AA   *Apostolicam actuositatem (Decree on the Apostolate of the Laity)*, 1965.

AG   *Ad gentes (Decree on the Missionary Activity of the Church)*, 1965.

CD   *Christus Dominus (Decree on the Pastoral Office of Bishops in the Church)*, 1965.

DV   *Dei Verbum (Dogmatic Constitution on Divine Revelation)*, 1965.

GS   *Gaudium et spes (Pastoral Constitution on the Church in the Modern World)*, 1965.

LG   *Lumen gentium (Dogmatic Constitution on the Church)*, 1964.

NA   *Nostra aetate (Declaration on the Church's Relation to Non-Christian Religions)*, 1965.

UR   *Unitatis redintegratio (Decree on Ecumenism)*, 1964.

Other Papal Documents

AL   *Amoris laetitia (The Joy of Love)*, Pope Francis, post-synodal apostolic exhortation, 2016.

CA   *Centesimus annus (On the Hundredth Anniversary of Rerum Novarum)*, Pope John Paul II, encyclical letter, 1991.

EG   *Evangelii gaudium (On the Proclamation of the Gospel in Today's World)*, Pope Francis, apostolic exhortation, 2013.

LS   *Laudato Si' (On Care for Our Common Home)*,
            Pope Francis, encyclical letter, 2015.

RM   *Redemptoris Missio (On the Permanent Validity
            of the Church's Miissionary Mandate)*, Pope John
            Paul II, encyclical letter, 1990.

Uus   *Ut unum sint (On Commitment to Ecumenism)*,
            Pope John Paul II, encyclical letter, 1995.

Documents of the
United States Conference of Catholic Bishops

*The Challenge of Peace: God's Promise and Our Response, A
    Pastoral Letter on War and Peace*, 1983

*Economic Justice for All: Pastoral Letter on Catholic Social
    Teaching and the US Economy*, 1986.

*Follow the Way of Love: US Bishops' Pastoral Message to
    Families*, Origins 23, no. 25 (December 2, 1993):
    433–43.

Index